Dedication

This book is dedicated to my mom and dad, my husband Tom, and my children Charlie and Catie.

Self Published in the United States of America

Cover photo credit: Tom Kiddoo
Cover and layout design: Kristine Go

BYE-POLAR

A Journey of Resilience, Power & Freedom

JULIE KIDDOO

Julie Kiddoo

Table of Contents

Acknowledgements

This book was made possible by all of the people who have ever listened to my stories of what I have gone through with my mental health. Those people who would say, "Julie, you need to write a book. Your story is so powerful. Others need to hear it so that they can heal too." And so I listened to all of the believers in my life and thus, Bye-Polar was born. It started out as a blog in 2015 and when I sat down to write for the first time the words kept pouring out of my head and onto the computer screen. Only after a few minutes I decided that I had too much to say for this to be a blog and so it became a book.

There are so many incredible people whom I would like to acknowledge for the creation of Bye-Polar. First to my family who has always been there for me. To my mom, Mary Jane McEachron, who never gave up in her pursuit to get me healthy. Without her, I would not be who I am today. And to my dad,

Mac McEachron, for being my rock. To my brother Charlie, for being there for me and loving me unconditionally. To my grandparents, Betty and Jim Junker and Betty and Edgar McEachron, and to all of my relatives, aunts, uncles cousins. I would not be where I am today without the love of my entire family. To my L (love), Tom Kiddoo, who puts up with me through thick and thin. To my children, Charlie and Catie, who give me purpose and a commitment to always seek the truth.

A special thank you to my sister-in-law Martha, for encouraging me to share my stories to empower others.

To all of the doctors, psychologists, psychiatrists and healers who have taken the time to get me better.

To all of my friends from my youth, Linda Lane, my friend since second grade, Sara Johnson Bailey, my closest friend in high school who was there when I crashed and on the other side when I woke up. To Kerrie Giesen, my dear friend from college who was always there for me through all of the ups and downs.

To my teacher, Baron Baptiste, for his commitment to being up to something bigger than himself and to sharing it with the planet and inspiring me to do the same. To The Baptiste Institute for creating life-changing programs that have saved my life and many others.

To my yoga teachers, Kelly Heath, Rachel Nelson, Jessa Munion, Amy Weintraub.

To the Community of Revolution Power Yoga, the teachers, ambassadors, and students. To the people who have participated in our yoga teacher trainings, workshops and yoga classes and have given me the gift of being able to share what I love.

To Rachel Delong for not taking no for an answer to going to a yoga class and for being a dear friend who always shows me that love is the way.

To the people who have given me an endless

supply of writing support. Holly Beavers for holding me accountable for three years to write every week and for editing this book three times. To Sandra Butler, who when traveling through Vail in 2017 asked me how my book was coming and I told her I wanted to delete it and she wouldn't let me. To Sandra for inspiring me to finish Bye-Polar for a bigger purpose and for all of the time she spent editing this book. To Kristine Go for offering to work with me to create the book cover and coaching me to think outside of the box all of the way up to the completion of this book.

To anyone who ever listened to my stories and encouraging me to share them with the world. Writing this book has been extremely cathartic and I am blessed for the opportunity to be able to express myself.

Introduction

I have dealt with anxiety and depression for more than 30 years. At the age of 17, I was diagnosed as Bipolar. I resigned myself to living with that label for many years. That is no longer the case and I decided to write a book to be a source of hope, inspiration and empowerment for those who deal or struggle with depression and/or anxiety or know someone who does. This book is a compilation of my own personal struggles with my mental health, coupled with healing tools that I have found along the way.

Please note that names of certain people in this book have been changed to protect their anonymity.

Bipolar Disorder Defined

*Definition of Bipolar Disorder adapted from the Mayo Clinic:

Bipolar Disorder, formerly called manic depression, causes extreme mood swings that include emotional highs (mania or hypomania) and lows (depression). An individual may become depressed, may feel sad or hopeless and lose interest or pleasure in most activities. When the mood shifts in the other direction, the individual may feel euphoric and full of energy. Mood shifts may occur only a few times a year or as often as several times a week.

*Definition of Bipolar Disorder from *https://www.seroquelxr.com:*

Bipolar Disorder is a mood disorder thought to be caused by chemical imbalances in the brain that can result in extreme swings in mood–from manic highs to depressive lows. The lows are Bipolar Depression and the highs are Bipolar Mania (see below). Bipolar Disorder is a lifelong condition that can affect both how an individual can feel and how they act. Symptoms of both Bipolar Depression and Bipolar Mania can cause problems for people with Bipolar Disorder. Some people report that Bipolar Depression tends to have a greater impact.

https://www.seroquelxr.com/bipolar-disorder/what-is-bipolar-disorder.html

Symptoms of Bipolar Depression From *https://www.seroquelxr.com:*

- Depressed mood most of the day; feeling sad or empty, tearful
- Significant loss of interest or pleasure in activities that used to be enjoyable
- Significant weight loss (when not dieting) or weight gain; decrease or increase in appetite
- Difficulty sleeping or sleeping too much

- Agitation or slowing down of thoughts and reduction in physical movements
- Fatigue or loss of energy
- Feelings of worthlessness or inappropriate guilt
- Poor concentration or having difficulty making decisions
- Thinking about death or suicide

https://www.seroquelxr.com/bipolar-disorder/bipolar-depression-symptoms.html

During a manic high, people feel unusually great. It's common to be overly talkative, have lots of energy, and need little sleep.

From WebMD on Symptoms of Mania:

- Have lots of energy
- Feel high or wired
- Have racing thoughts
- Talk fast
- Take more risks
- Need less sleep than usual to feel rested

- Have more distractions than usual
- Have intense senses, such as smell and touch

First Experience with Depression

I attended a small private Pre-Kindergarten through Twelfth grade school in Golden Valley, Minnesota-Breck School. Something really cool that my high school had was a program called May Program. It was similar to J-term (the January break that colleges have) except that it was in May. It was for three weeks and one could choose to take various classes at school, go on a trip abroad that the school planned, or one could create his or her own work study.

At the end of my Sophomore year in 1986, when I was 16, I took part in May Program. I went to Wausau, Wisconsin and stayed with my grama McEachron for three weeks to work (volunteer) with preschool children at Wausau Child Care, a child care organization my grama started in 1968. When I was a Freshman in high school I had volunteered in our school's preschool classroom and I loved it, and that is why I chose to do my May Program at the

Wausau Child Care.

As much as I enjoyed working at the pre-school, I started to experience my first symptoms of depression. I remember being in my grama's guest room, looking around, feeling alone, and thinking of going off to college. The thought of going to college and being alone and not knowing how to take care of myself scared the crap out me. I started to not sleep well and my appetite went out the window. I remember feeling a pit in my stomach. I wasn't quite sure why I was feeling this way, I just knew that I felt off.

Why was I not sleeping well? Why did my stomach feel upset? Why did I not have an appetite? I loved food. I know that I was missing my friends. After being at Breck since a Freshman I finally felt as though I had made some really neat friendships. I think I was worried I was missing out and that my friends would forget about me. It was almost a feeling of not fitting in while I was gone.

My grama and I went to Door County, Wisconsin as a weekend getaway while I stayed with her. I felt like I couldn't even enjoy the beautiful place we were in because I was feeling so low.

After the three weeks were over I went back home. I continued to feel a little funky. My mom took me to see Dr. Barnes, our family's pediatrician, to see if there was anything he could do for me. I don't remember much of what he said other than that how I was feeling was normal and that it would most likely pass.

Once I got into the groove with my friends for the summer I was back to my usual self. Time healed that one.

The Fall of Significant Change

Change has always been a big trigger for me. The change of seasons, going back to school in the fall, and oh, the fall--that was the worst season of all. The days would get shorter and shorter, less light would be available during the days and the impending fear of the winter was practically suffocating.

It was fall of 1987. I was 17 and a senior in high school. At the beginning of October my mom took me on a college trip to visit the University of Puget Sound in Tacoma, Washington. The weather was gorgeous, despite how much rain they typically get. I got to stay in a sorority house with one of my friends, Kelly, who was two years older than me. We went to fraternity parties, stayed up late and had so much fun. The second day I was there I got a tour of the college campus--old brick buildings, lots of cool amenities, really nice people.

The second night there something strange

started happening. I lost my appetite and I couldn't sleep. My heart was racing. I felt scared. I was terrified at the thought of going off to college, even though it wouldn't happen for almost another year.

My mom and I flew back to Minnesota at the end of the weekend and by Monday I was back in school. Except there was one huge problem. My body was there, my mind and spirit were not. I still wasn't sleeping very well and my appetite was out the window. I couldn't concentrate at school.

My mom took me to a psychologist named Dr. Sweat. She was short and fat. The only good thing I remember was that she said the word 'should' is a bad word as it creates guilt and is disempowering. Other than that I don't think she did much for me.

By the end of October my parents pulled me out of school, as I was so depressed and school just wasn't working for me. I was having such a hard time as I could not concentrate. The depression had completely taken over my body and mind. Some of my friends have shared with me recently that I was just blank. One even said that I had such a blank stare on my face that I seemed scary to her. She said it wasn't even like I was Julie.

At the time I didn't want to talk to any of my friends, because I was worried about what they would think of me. I didn't want to 'ruin' any of my friendships, so I just shut them out. I hung out with my parents at home. I was scared and alone. I remember telling my mom one day that I thought I was retarded. I couldn't remember anything. My mind felt blank.

Shortly after seeing Dr. Sweat, my mom took me to Dr. Barnes, our family's pediatrician to get his professional opinion on what to do with me. Dr. Barnes was able to get us an appointment with Dr. Smith, a psychiatrist at Abbott Northwestern, a hospital near downtown Minneapolis.

Dr. Smith was my first of many psychiatrists.

Dr. Smith was a wonderful and kind man. I really liked him. He put me on an antidepressant, Pamelor and Xanax, an anti-anxiety drug. I started feeling better, the clouds started to lift, my appetite came back and I was able to sleep better. Yay! I was supposed to return to school after Thanksgiving.

Then, I am not sure what happened, the tides turned and the depression came back with full force. I had a panic attack. I couldn't breathe. I was in such bad shape. The only thing I could really do was get myself dressed.

My dad said that watching me go through the depression was as hard as losing his dad, my grandfather. He said that because I was having a hard time sleeping he slept in our guest room which was right next door to my room. He said that I would wake up several times a night (I don't think I ever slept) and would be shaking and so he would just hold me to calm me down.

Since I was too depressed to go back to school

after Thanksgiving I went to Wausau, Wisconsin with my cousin Sandra and her newborn son, Max, to see our grandma. It was that week that I stopped talking.

Willow Street

It was December 9th, 1987: a day I have since come to embrace. My parents didn't know what they could do for me. I wasn't getting any better; I was getting worse. So they did what they thought was best for me and admitted me into the Willow Street Mental Health Hospital in Loring Park, Minneapolis. The facility where I stayed was on the second floor. It was a place that was really meant for teenagers who had a drug or alcohol problem.

I remember the first night I was at Willow Street like it was yesterday. There was a front desk to the right after getting off the elevators. My room was at the beginning of the hall that was to the right of the desk on the left side of the hall. I had a roommate, although I do not remember her name. I had my Teddy Bear and my bedspread from home with me. The only thing I could remember besides my name was my social security number. I felt blank.

I felt totally alone and scared. How long was I going to be here? Would I ever get out? Would I ever feel normal again? I didn't even know what normal was since I had been so depressed for over two months. What was real? What wasn't real?

The people who worked at Willow Street thought I was suicidal, so they put me on suicide watch. The first night I was in bed at Willow Street someone kept coming into the room to check on me and would shine a flashlight on me. I'm not sure if they thought I was going to slit my wrists or what. Throughout all of the depression and anxiety I experienced I was actually never suicidal, but Willow Street didn't know that so they took all necessary precautions to make sure I was safe.

I had been taken cold turkey off the Pamelor and Xanax I was taking. Xanax is not a drug to be taken lightly. The withdrawal symptoms I was experiencing were horrific. I felt delusional. I felt pins and needles. I was sweating and felt nauseous and dizzy. I felt like my scalp was going to come away from my head. My heart was racing. Where was I? I felt like someone had a gun to my head.

I got worse after being admitted to Willow Street. The second day I was in Willow Street they moved me into a different room without a roommate. I became catatonic (catatonia is a mental stupor in which one cannot move). I couldn't function. I couldn't get out of bed. It seemed as though the nurses were getting mad at me for not getting out of bed. Was I faking it?

At some point I got out of bed. I remember being next to the front desk and I wet my pants. I was too numb to even feel humiliated. A nurse took me into the bathroom and gave me a bath. It was actually the first time since being in Willow Street that I felt nurtured.

That day the heavy drugs came: Haldol, Thorazine, Klonopin.

My dad told me that when he and my mom

visited me in the hospital all I would do is just stare at the ceiling. I wouldn't talk. I wouldn't make eye contact. I couldn't do anything. Oh, and then the therapy started: Family Therapy with Dr. Fred, Movement Therapy, Occupational Therapy.

I went to Family Therapy with my parents and my brother and Dr. Fred, the family therapist at Willow Street. My dad and I had always done a lot of things together while I was growing up. Dr. Fred accused my dad of molesting me or at least implied that there was sexual abuse. That didn't go over so well with any of us--just not the case. After that accusation we all stopped seeing Dr. Fred. My mom had a phone conversation with Dr. Fred and gave him feedback as to why we weren't going to see him anymore. As an adult I had lunch with my dad and asked him about the family sessions with Dr. Fred and how he had implied that there was sexual abuse. At that lunch when my dad was telling me about Dr. Fred he said, "Fuck this I am outta here." I can say for a fact my dad never laid a hand on me...ever!

I had a really happy childhood. On the outside, everything was perfect. I had two parents who had a loving relationship with each other and still do after fifty plus years of marriage. They were always there for me both physically and emotionally. My mom was a stay-at-home mom and although my dad worked and traveled a lot for work, he always spent quality time with me when he was home. We rode horses, we hiked, we played softball, we traveled together. More on my childhood in the next chapter.

I had my fair share of psychiatrists while I was at Willow Street. Once I was admitted, my first shrink was Dr. Marshall. She was amazing. I still think of her today. It was Dr. Marshall who labeled me Bipolar. My mom said that maybe the reason Marshall thought I could be Bipolar is because the antidepressant (Pamelor) didn't work and could have actually brought out a Bipolar episode. I don't think my parents told me this diagnosis at the time, as my memory of being told I was Bipolar came a little over a year later.

At a time when I felt absolutely no hope, she gave us all the hope we needed. She told my parents "Julie will graduate from high school, she will graduate from college, she will get married and she will have kids." Even though I couldn't see it at the time, I clung on to those words of hope for a long time. And against all odds, I graduated from high school, graduated from college, got married and have two beautiful kids. More on this later.

I was eventually put on Lithium, a drug intended for Bipolar patients. I couldn't stand the side effects of being on that medication. The Lithium made my teeth feel so weird. I had a horrible metallic taste in my mouth and my teeth felt like they were going to fall out. Eating felt weird. I was so puffy. My face didn't even look like me. I had no clue who I was. I didn't know which end was up. I only knew my name and my social security number.

Because I was so depressed I had to eat the majority of my meals on the unit floor, even though the kitchen was on the ground level. I do remember getting to eat a few meals downstairs from time to time. It was such a treat getting to ride the elevator up and down, as it meant I got to get off the second floor and have a change of scenery.

The good news though is that at some point while I was at Willow Street the clouds started to lift and I began to feel better and made some friends. My first friend was Sally. She was thin with long legs, long blonde hair and blue eyes that were hidden behind glasses. I can't remember why she was in there. When we started to feel better we would run up and down the hall together.

I don't even think we got any kind of physical exercise. I just remember doing occupational therapy where we made nice things out of leather or ceramics. I also went to movement therapy where I had to pretend that a chair was my mother. The therapist made me yell at the chair to imitate yelling at my mother. That felt so fucked up. Pretending a chair was my mom. She wasn't even the problem. Supposedly I had a chemical imbalance. Who knows? Or was the depression situational and an isolated event? Was change really the trigger for me? I was molested when I was 7 which I now know had a huge impact on my mental health. More details on this in the The Healing Begins chapter.

The other two friends I remember were John and Beth. Beth told me that she and her mom were in the lobby of Willow Street while I was being admitted and they both thought that I had an eating disorder because I was so thin. I became thin as my depression suppressed my appetite, not because I had an issue with my body image. And I had such a huge crush on John. He was so cute. Kind of a naughty boy though. Which probably made him even more attractive. I think he was in Willow Street because he had a drinking problem. And at the end of the day it really didn't matter why someone was in there, we were all in there for some reason or another. And we all hoped that we would get the hell out of there. Eventually, when we did get out of there, I got together with my Willow Street friends again, especially Sally. She was the saving grace of Willow Street. It was nice being with people who knew what it was like to be hospitalized, to miss school and to reintegrate into society.

Released

I was at Willow Street for two months and three days. I was released February 12th, 1988, the day before my 18th birthday. I was able to go home during the day on Christmas Eve and on Christmas Day. I wasn't allowed to spend the nights at home. It was so hard having to go back to the hospital and I am sure even harder for my parents.

In a recent conversation with my brother, he said he remembers the day I came home from the hospital, watching me get out of the car and walking to the house. He said I was walking really slowly and gingerly, just like someone who had been hospitalized for surgery.

Once I was released I had to attend an outpatient program at Willow Street that I went to five days a week for two weeks. For the following two weeks after that I did a combination of half days at school and half days of doing the outpatient at school and half days of doing the outpatient program at Willow Street. I don't even remember the first day I went back to school. I think I have blocked it out of my memory to protect myself.

I know that going back to school after having been so depressed, hospitalized and on several medications was extremely difficult for me. I had been out of school for two quarters. I had missed half of my senior year. I was supposed to be the captain of my alpine ski team and missed that. There was a lot I missed. I knew though, in my heart of hearts, how important it was for me to graduate with my peers. Fortunately, because I was such an overachiever, I had more than enough credits from my previous years in high school to be able to graduate on time.

I graduated from Breck School in May 1988. Since I missed the majority of the college application processes, I applied to the College of St. Thomas, a small private Catholic college in St. Paul, Minnesota, which is now called the University of St. Thomas.

I remember the application was a two sided piece of blue paper. The application was super easy to fill out. Thank God since I couldn't really focus on much.

The summer after I graduated from high school was a rough one for our family. I had always done the 'right thing' growing up. In the past I never really defied my parents. That summer as I started to feel better mentally I also starting breaking away from and rebelling against my parents. I wanted to be and feel normal and yet I was hurting inside. It was hard on my parents. I was so dependent on them my senior year of high school and then suddenly I was rebelling. I remember cashing a twenty dollar check that I received for graduation and going to a gas station to buy a pack of cigarettes and a 'shit happens' key chain.

One afternoon my mom must have suspected that I had been smoking and she came running after me in our driveway. I ran down our driveway with two cigarettes and a lighter in my hand. I think I threw everything in my underwear. By the time I ran far enough, I felt guilty and threw the stuff in the woods. Later I picked it up: couldn't waste two smokes!

Now that I am a mother I see the torture I put my mother through that summer of 1988. I was scared. I so desperately wanted to be 'normal.' I was hurting. I felt shame. And I had fun.

Childhood

I had an extraordinarily happy childhood. My mom was a stay-at-home mom and was very involved with my younger brother, Charlie, and me. I remember taking trips to the grocery store and always getting a box of animal crackers while we shopped. It seemed like the coolest thing ever. One grocery store we would go to, Lund's, had a donut maker and we would watch them make donuts for what seemed like hours. I am sure I got to partake in eating them from time to time as well.

I was born in Edina, Minnesota (a town neighboring Minneapolis). From birth to the age of 7 I lived in Minneapolis in a brick house with a big red door that was a block away from Lake Harriet. There were many lakes near where I lived and my dad would put me on the back of his bike and ride around those lakes every Saturday. I remember him getting mad at me because I would fall asleep and when my head bobbed, it would throw him off balance. It kind of became a joke.

I had lots of friends in that neighborhood in Minneapolis: my best childhood friend was Sara Newhall. She and I did everything together--we even dressed the same. Back in those days we walked to school together.

When I was 7 my parents built a house in Medina, Minnesota, in the country thirty minutes west of Minneapolis. I remember feeling so sad to leave the neighborhood and my friends. The country was pretty cool though. We had twenty acres of land, a pool, a barn, two horses and a mean Shetland pony, dogs, cats, hamsters, guinea pigs, ducks, fish and who knows what else.

My parents spent a ton of time with me, particularly my dad, despite traveling a lot for his work. He always made our time together count. He and I would go horseback riding together, play catch with the softball, take ski trips out to Vail, Colorado and many more amazing things. We also went on lots of family trips with my mom, dad and my brother: Hawaii every spring break, Steamboat to ski at Christmas time and usually a fun trip in the summer to Canada or Montana. I had everything under the moon--the love of two devoted parents, tons of travel, financial stability, well provided for, a great house, new clothes and the list could go on and on.

Our family life was pretty ideal. Of course there were plenty of the normal dysfunctional familial things, such as us kids getting yelled at or my mom and dad raising their voices at each other. We were far from perfect and I guess what I am trying to convey is that we were very 'normal.' There wasn't any abuse in my family. Our parents spent tons of time with us. My dad was always quick to praise. And yet as 'normal and happy' as my childhood was I still ended up going through a major depression. It didn't matter that I came from a 'nice' family, was well provided for, had the love of two adoring parents.

When I started going down the path of depression my senior year of high school, no amount of doing fun things, shopping, travel, exercise, helped me. I was in a funk and someone on the outside would think it was for no good reason. Other than my emotions being triggered by change and the fear of going off to college, I didn't know why I went into such a deep depression. Now, with the knowledge I have gained through the work I have done, I see the connection between my mental health and sexual abuse as I had a pivotal experience when I was 7 years old. I also had other experiences that were contributing factors as I will share in the pages ahead.

The Molestation

As I mentioned earlier, my parents built a house in Medina, Minnesota, a small town out in the country. Since our new house wasn't finished when we moved out of Minneapolis, we rented a townhouse in Wayzata, a town just ten minutes east of where our new abode was being built. The town homes were right next to Highway 12, which later became known as I-394. They were up on a small hill and there were four large buildings that made up the town home complex.

At these townhomes my brother, Charlie, met his lifelong best friend, Colin. Those two were always together and I thought of them as double trouble. We also had neighbors, the Jones. The parents were Rita and Floyd and they had three kids, Paul who was fourteen, Tina who was 7 years old like me, and a third, whose name or age I don't remember.

Paul used to babysit my brother and me. I

remember we'd be hanging out in my room and he would put his hands down my pants and rub my butt. I thought he was just giving me affection. I was always warned by my parents to never talk to a stranger, never to take candy from a stranger and never get in the car with a stranger. I was never told to watch out for inappropriate touching as sexual misconduct. I don't blame my parents for not warning me that there were people out there that did this sort of thing. Sexual abuse just wasn't talked about back then like it is now, and my parents had no idea what was going on.

Anyway, without any kind of force Paul took my pants off and tried having sex with me. A 7 year old vagina really doesn't make a great host for a fourteen year old's penis. I don't think he ever penetrated, but he did ejaculate. I know this happened at least two or three times at my house. And I remember one time when we were at his house. He played a 'game' with his sister Tina and me. He would have us hide in the bathroom and then one at a time he would take us and do 'his thing' with us. I think that was the last time that he had any contact with me, as we moved into our new house in Medina shortly after this happened.

I kept this a secret from my parents for ten years. The crazy thing is that while all of that was going on, I never felt scared. I never felt forced. The way Paul went about his thing was actually very gentle and he made it seem like a reward. Since I never knew being touched inappropriately was bad, I never said anything. When I was in high school I told my friends what had happened and they all said I should tell someone. I am not sure why I never did. I think I didn't want to deal with it. And I know that I had a hard time expressing my feelings, which is a big reason why I went through the depression. Coming out of family therapy at Willow Street, Dr. Fred once said, "Julie needs to learn to express herself." He was right--maybe the only thing he was right about.

Paul was a grocery bagger at Lund's grocery store. When I was in high school I went shopping with my mom one day; we were checking out and Paul was our bagger. My mom said, "Julie, you remember Paul, don't you?" I just remember looking at him. I don't even think I said anything. I didn't remember feeling angry, but I certainly remembered him. I just thought he was creepy. The more I shared with my friends about what happened with Paul, the more they made me realize that what he did was wrong. My friends wanted me to report him to the police and I wanted nothing to do with that. Back then I would never express myself. I just kept everything inside.

My mom on occasion would ask me, "Did Paul Jones wet the bed?" I knew why she was asking me that as a child; the bed was wet from Paul ejaculating, but she did not know that. I asked her recently why she kept asking me and she said because the bed was wet. She said she never put two and two together. My answer was always no to the bed wetting question when my mom would ask me until the fall of 1987 when I was in the throes of my severe depression. I was in my bedroom and my mom was asking me questions about things that could have possibly contributed to my depression. "Have you smoked pot?" Yes, I replied. "Why would you do that, you know it's not good for you?" I know but I did it anyway. "Did Paul wet the bed?" My response was finally "Yes."

So finally, after ten years went on, I told my mother the whole story and left nothing out. I can't imagine as a mother finding out ten years later that my daughter had gone through something like this and never knowing. I know she felt awful: riddled with guilt. For me it was such a relief to finally be able to tell my mom the truth after hiding it for so long. Allowing this experience to surface and healing from it are covered in more detail in the chapters: *The Healing Begins, Healing the Past and A World of Possibilites.*

The Attack

In August of 1986, when I was 16, I traveled to Colorado with my high school friend, Christy Bieber. Her parents owned a ranch in Paonia, a teeny, tiny little town in western Colorado. The surroundings were absolutely gorgeous. Rolling mountains covered with green grass, horses roaming in the pasture, land that went on for miles.

Christy and I decided that we wanted to do a backpacking trip, just the two of us, so we set off for an overnight trip, huge packs and all. We had been hiking all day and searching for the base of Mt. Lamborn. "Mount Lamborn is a mountain summit in the West Elk Mountains range of the Rocky Mountains of North America. The 11,402-foot peak is located in Gunnison National Forest, south of the town of Paonia in Delta County, Colorado. The summit of Mount Lamborn is the highest point in Delta County. It lies at the western edge of the West Elks, rising dramatically nearly 6,000 ft above the valley of the North Fork Gunnison River to the west." (From Wikipedia). Christy had been to the top of Lamborn about fifteen times previously, but we went to a location around the back side where neither of us had been before. I don't even think we had a map.

Christy and I hiked all day and we were getting really tired. We had been bushwhacking (off trail) much of the day. We realized we were lost and could not find a trail. We could hear someone chopping wood in the distance. At this point we were in thick brush with tall trees and low shrubs surrounding us. We followed the sound of the wood chopping and came upon two men from Mexico who didn't speak a word of English. We tried asking them where the trail to Mt. Lamborn was. They shrugged their heads and pointed in an uphill direction.

As Christy and I walked away we thought it was so weird that these guys were working and living in the United States and didn't speak any English (we were clueless teenagers to think this at the time). So onward we hiked. My round, striped canteen was clanking against my chest. Sweat was crusted all over my face and I felt too pooped to pop.

Eventually we found the trail only to look up and see the same men, this time on horses. They each were on a horse and had a third horse behind them tied to a rope. With hand gestures and mumbling we were able to discern that they were offering us a ride. Even though it sounded quite lovely to hitch a ride at this point, we declined. The men continued going up the pass and Christy and I continued to hike up the path behind them. They had a male dog that kept humping Christy's Golden Retriever. The men laughed at this. Christy and I felt awkward and were mad at the dog.

We needed to get to the top of the pass and down the other side of it, as that was where the base of Mt. Lamborn was and then we could set up our tent for the night. I just remember feeling so worn out. ‘Just put one foot in front of the other’ was all I kept saying to myself.

We hiked for about another hour, the sun getting lower in the sky. At last we reached the top of the pass. Once we arrived at the top of the pass the two men were there with their horses again. This time they were standing on the ground. The men walked toward us and I thought they were congratulating us for making it to the top of the pass. Man was I wrong.

They attacked us. The guy who attacked me first put his hand on my shoulder and then got me down on the ground on my back. I still had my backpack on with a chest and a hip strap keeping it tied to my body. I was struggling to get this guy off of me, but he was winning. He was on his knees. I was trying to punch him in the nuts through his jeans. He unzipped my pants and started to finger my vagina while my pants were still on. I kept saying to myself ‘this can’t be happening, this isn’t happening.’ I could hear Christy screaming. At one point she said, "Julie, get the knife." I think I said something like "I'm trying." Getting the knife wasn't an option with this man on top of me and my knife in the top part of my backpack. It seemed as though Christy had more of a fight left in her than I did. She remained on her feet longer than I did but eventually was knocked down and cursing that her backpack was still on her back.

I kept trying to roll over so that I could get away from him. I just remember thinking 'Oh my God we are going to get raped and we are going to die.' I was encapsulated with fear like I had never been in my entire life. It was such a helpless feeling.

As I kept trying to roll to my right side, I finally succeeded. I was able to roll onto my side and get away. These two men were sheep herders and their boss came up the other side of the pass. Once the men saw their boss, they ran off into the woods with their horses and that is how Christy and I became free from the attack. The boss said he wasn't going to come up the pass until the next day, but he thought he heard a bear and a deer fighting. Instead he heard Christy and me screaming for our lives. Thank God he came up there that afternoon or Christy and I would have been dead or close to it.

The boss man had a horse and let Christy and me ride on it to the bottom of the other side of the pass. The man didn't say much other than, "It's not like these boys to do something like that." For some reason we trusted this man, probably because the men ran away when they saw him.

The man led us on his horse down to his camp where he just dropped us off. He never offered to take us all the way home. He was far from kind, but ended up being our savior. Without even speaking about it, we knew that camping out that night was not an option. We set off back toward her parents ranch house which was still a few miles away. We did our two day hike in one.

Of course the heavens opened up and it started

pouring rain. At this point we started running down the dirt road, which quickly turned into mud from the rain. Our shoes were caked with so much mud it looked like we had mud snowshoes on. It was like a scene out of a movie. I don't remember us saying much to each other about what had happened on our cold, wet run home. I think we were both in shock and just wanted to get back to a dry, safe place. At last we arrived at the ranch, just before the sun said goodbye for the night. What a long, hard day!

When we got back to the ranch we told her parents what happened. Christy's parents originally thought we came home early because we got into a fight with each other. Once her parents learned what happened her dad called the sheriff to report it. The sheriff came over to the house that night and we filled out a report telling the story of what had happened. Apparently, the following day the police went up to arrest the men and the men shot at them before turning themselves in. Christy and I were so lucky that we weren't shot and killed.

Before we went backpacking I started to feel that same weird, funky depression feeling I experienced when I was in Wausau with my grama in May of that year. I am not sure why I was feeling funky before the backpacking trip. Then after we got attacked I felt really off. I couldn't sleep and didn't have much of an appetite.

Christy's parents must have called my parents that night to let them know what had happened. My parents came to pick me up the next day and they took me to Snowmass, Colorado, a mountain town an hour and a half from Paonia, where I could begin to heal. My parents and I spent a few mellow days in Snowmass, digesting what had happened before we went back home. I remember my mom saying to me that this wouldn't happen again. That I was done with that (the bad thing that happened).

After a few days in Snowmass we went back home and into 'normal summer.' Life really continued on as though nothing had happened. My mom said she took me to my pediatrician, Dr. Barnes, to get checked out and he told my mom that unless I talked about the attack there was nothing to do about it. I know if that happened in this day and age I would have been marched right into therapy. Or at least that is what I would have my kids do if, God forbid, something like that happened to them. And I know in 1986 my mom and everyone did the best they could with what they knew how to do.

That fall of 1986 Christy and I and our moms flew out to Gunnison, Colorado, to go to court to testify against our attackers. Gunnison is located in Gunnison County, neighboring Delta county where Paonia is located. I remember feeling scared to face our attackers in the courtroom. What was I going to say? Would I be heard?

Our lawyer said the attackers had shaved, had a haircut and wore nice clothes. I am pretty sure I would not have been able to identify them. Fortunately or unfortunately, I can't decide which, we did not testify in the courtroom. We ended up settling outside of the courtroom with a plea bargain. The men got deported back to Mexico with a slap on the wrists and that was it. Didn't really seem like a fair punishment at the time. And yet, the whole ordeal was over and it was time to move on.

After being in Gunnison for a few days we flew back to Minnesota and life went on as 'normal.' I don't recall ever consciously thinking about getting attacked. It was something of the past.

Readmitted

The fall of 1988 I was 18 and a freshman at the College of St. Thomas in St. Paul, Minnesota. I had survived the summer of 1988 probably by the seat of my pants. With a full perm on my head I began my freshman year. Since I had hit my depression one year prior I had created the thought in my mind that I hated fall. The days were shorter and darker and the sense of impending doom was looming as winter was coming. There was a fear of the unknown. Despite my dislike of the fall, things initially seemed to be going fine. I was plugging along in school, making new friends, dabbling in a little partying, and was still shy as hell though.

October of 1988 I saw Dr. Smith, shrink # 1 in my life, and for some reason he took me off the lithium pills. He must have thought I was in a really good place. I remember taking my pills into the bathroom at my dorm and flushing them down the toilet. It was a happy day for me.

As time rolled on that fall and I was nearing December 9th--the one year anniversary of being hospitalized--I started getting what I call a little crazy. I felt nervous, I felt manic. I remember people telling me to shut up as I wouldn't stop talking.

My parents went out of town for a weekend at the end of November and I watched my brother and his friend, Colin. I was so irritable. I remember chasing my brother through the house and he closed a door that I was running through--I hit the door with the side of my arm and the next thing I knew I was on the ground and had passed out. Charlie was standing next to me saying, "Julie, are you okay? What happened?"

I wasn't really sure what happened. All I knew is just that I felt nuttier than a shithouse rat. I went back to college after that weekend and continued in school with my excessive talking and manic behavior.

On the night of December 9th I felt scared

when I went to bed. My heart was racing. I felt alone and didn't know what to do. I called the campus security and one of the guards came to my room. I remember lying in my bed as he sat in my desk chair and telling him my whole story of depression and being hospitalized the year prior. I think he was crying too, not sure though. I have no idea why I called security--I wasn't suicidal. I think I just felt really scared.

Someone from school must have called my parents as the next day they picked me up and took me home. I was in no state to be in school. I remember being really mad at my mom, though. I blamed her for everything that I had gone through. I have no idea why I blamed her. I was just mad. Up until this point I had never blamed my mom for anything. I think I just wanted to be a 'normal" college student and didn't want to be protected and I was resisting her protection. Geez--how nice--especially now that I am a mom--it sucks I did that and I guess I had to blame my mental health on someone.

My mom called her shrink, Dr. Channing, (who ended up becoming mine too). He was the best shrink out of all of the ones I had! My memory was that Dr. Channing told her over the phone that I was officially Bipolar. According to my mom, I was labeled Bipolar by Dr. Marshall when I was admitted to Willow Street. On a side note I was taking psychology 101 that fall and was failing nonetheless. When I was told I was Bipolar the definition of depression I learned in that psychology class kept filling my mind--'has a sense of never-ending impending doom.' That was how I felt.

Even though my mom had called Dr. Channing for his advice she took me back to Dr. Smith. He put me back on lithium again, I guess since it worked the first time, despite my feeling icky on it. That's when the real crazy started to come out. I went back to college for a little while and then when I couldn't deal with anything anymore I went back home with my parents.

I was not getting any better. I was getting worse. My mania was increasing and nothing was making any sense.

My parents took me to see Dr. Channing that December. We arrived at Abbott Northwestern Hospital and I went into what looked like the emergency room to see Dr. Channing. The next thing I knew I was being admitted to Abbott Northwestern's Mental Health unit. This unit was for adults as opposed to Willow Street which was for juveniles. My memory of being admitted is pretty fuzzy, although I do remember when the intake nurse asked me why I was there I said because of my mother. How nice, I was blaming my mother when she was the very person who was always there for me.

While we were in the car headed to Minneapolis to see the doctor, my mania and delusions created an entire fantasy that my Breck friends were throwing a huge reunion for me at the Metrodome (home of the Minnesota Vikings and The Minnesota

Twins, at the time). There was going to be a parade and Princess Di and Prince Charles were coming into town. All of this was for me. Talk about eating a piece of humble pie. Gulp!

In addition to the huge party that my friends were throwing for me at the Metrodome, I told myself I was getting married to a childhood friend, Mark. One time when the nurse came in to check on me during my first night at Abbott I was convinced that she was bringing in my cousin Sandra's wedding dress and putting it in the locked closet that was in my room. The fantasy went on for three days.

When I was admitted to Abbott I was taken cold turkey off lithium. Three days after I was taken off lithium, I still had toxic levels of it in my system. I had an allergic reaction to the drug and my body and mind were fighting it.

I was placed on Tegretol, a drug that was originally intended for people with epilepsy. As a side-benefit, it is also a mood stabilizer. The drug was great. I had no side effects and felt great the entire time I was on it. I had to get my blood checked monthly and Dr. Channing said that if I ever wanted kids I would have to wean off of it.

This round of hospitalization only lasted for two weeks instead of two months. I got to do occupational therapy where we made some cool things--right in time for Christmas. I was released on Christmas Eve. My college had J-term, (a 4 week break in January) so I didn't have to go back to school until the end of January 1989. My mom begged me not to go back to school. I think she was worried that I would get teased and that people would judge me since I had been such a nut case in December. What would people think? I know she was just trying to protect me.

Life in College

When J-term was over in January of 1989 I went back to college. In between my episodes of depression and mania, I was always so determined to be 'normal,' whatever normal was. I was not going to let anything get in my way. My senior year of high school after I was hospitalized I was determined to go back to Breck and complete my senior year. I was determined to go to college. So of course I went back. I never got teased (at least not to my face). Everything worked out just fine.

The summer of 1989 I got a job at Brookstone, a gadget store in the Ridgedale Mall in Minnetonka, Minnesota. There I made several friends, my best one being my friend Maria. We named our group of friends The Brookstone Gang and went out every Saturday night during college.

I ended up transferring to the University of Minnesota in the fall of 1989. The College of St.

Thomas started to feel too small for me. Perhaps I was paranoid about what others thought of me. I felt ready for a change and to meet new people. I moved in an apartment on Elm Street, just off campus with my friend Kim from high school and her friend Anne Marie.

January of 1990 I went through winter rush to join a sorority (rush is a sorority recruitment process in which university undergraduate women join a sorority). Since the University of Minnesota was so big my dad encouraged me to join a sorority. He was in a fraternity in college. He said if you only meet one friend, then that's all that matters.

I joined Tri-Delta, Delta Delta Delta. It was perfect--right in the glory days when Saturday Night Live would make fun of Tri-Delta. "Delta Delta Delta can I help ya help ya help ya???" Then of course the cheer we made up went on to say, "Delta Delta Delta can I help ya help ya help ya??? Man on the doorstep all night. Don't try the others, Tri-Delt."

I made lots of great friends at Tri-Delt, my two best friends being Kerrie and Ellen. Kerrie has been a lifesaver: one who knows me inside and out and one who has pulled me out of many dark times. Truly a friend for life. Ellen and I instantly clicked over skiing and she became my ski buddy and still is.

Life through college, like anything, had its ups and downs. In September of 1990 I went to Italy with my Brookstone friend, Maria, and her mother. It was a fun trip and also had its share of up and downs. Shortly after we returned from Italy we had to rush into getting ready as college was starting soon.

A Bump in the Road

Remember at the beginning of the book when I said that change was always a trigger for me? Well, I didn't give myself enough time to transition from being back from Europe before school started and I could feel myself slipping into a funk. My sleep and appetite went out the window, despite the fact that I was on Tegretol. I was supposed to move into the sorority house and I just couldn't do it. As much as I loved my sorority sisters, the thought of living with forty of them when I felt depressed didn't seem like a great idea. So I ended up getting an apartment with Maria and her high school friend, Mari.

The depression was fogging my days. I would cry myself to sleep at night. I knew something wasn't right so I went to Dr. Channing. He put me on Prozac for a few months to lift the fog in addition to the Tegretol I was already taking. It worked, by golly. The fog lifted after a week or so and I was feeling like my old self again.

I learned from that experience that I needed to give myself adequate time to transition. To tell myself on future trips 'you are going to need a couple of days to come down from your trip and transition back into life.' I still mentally prepare myself to be gentle and kind when I come back from a trip and not to race back into life. I also organize the hell out of my life before I go anywhere--from work stuff to emptying all of the trash cans in the house so that when I return home it can be as smooth as possible. I can't always choose the things that happen around me; however, I can choose how I respond and I can organize the small stuff, which in turn eases my mental health.

After the experience of going on Prozac for a few months, my mental health was pretty stable. By now, I knew change was a perpetual struggle for me. We were on the quarter system in college so three times during the school year my classes and my schedule would change.

For the first two to three weeks of each quarter I was a basket case, trying to juggle a new schedule. And then I would get into the swing of things and everything would be okay.

Since I was taking Tegretol, I had to get my blood checked once a month, specifically for my thyroid. Spring of 1991 one of my tests came back indicating that my thyroid was low, so I was sent to a specialist, Dr. Midas. He was awful. He always ran late. When we would come into the room he would have stacks of paper he'd ruffle through and say, "Wait, what's your name?" He was completely impersonal. At any rate he said, "You have a hypothyroid and I am going to put you on Synthroid, a drug to regulate your thyroid." I was so upset. The last fucking thing I wanted to do was to take another fucking pill. After getting back to my apartment from filling my prescription, I chucked the bag with the pill bottle in it across the room. I was sad and mad and was completely having a pity party. Despite my resistance, I began taking the pills which caused me to have horrible acne.

Summer of 1991 was the first summer that I worked at The YMCA of the Rockies in Estes Park, Colorado with my bestie, Kerrie. While I was working at the Y-Camp kids would say to me, "Ew! Why do you have pepperoni all over your face?" Parents were so embarrassed. In the kids' defense, my skin was pretty scary looking as it was riddled with acne. Kids just say it like it is. No filter. It was so humiliating to have such awful acne.

Despite being covered with zits all over my face, I made some incredible friends that summer. It felt great, despite how I looked, that people actually wanted to be my friend. Well, I have to admit that Kerrie and I were pretty darn fun, even though chubby and zitty.

After my first summer in Estes, it was determined that I actually didn't have a hypothyroid. Tegretol can mask the accurate reading for thyroid in blood work. Dr. Midas said no way did the synthroid cause that bad acne. I beg to differ. My feeling at the time was that I got all those zits for nothing. Looking back now, I see that having to live with such horrible acne and still making great connections taught me that people loved me for who I was and not what I looked like.

At some point the following spring I went to the dermatologist since my acne hadn't fully recovered and took Accutane for five months. I had to swear on my life--up one side and down the other--to the doctor's office that I wouldn't get pregnant while taking this medication due to possible birth defects. I was like, "I haven't even had sex yet, not like it's going to happen now." The people at the dermatologist office said, "Oh you never know, you might start feeling good about yourself..." Sex didn't happen.

Heading West

I graduated from college in the spring of 1994. It had always been my plan to take a "year off after college." Summer of '94 was my fourth summer working at The YMCA of the Rockies in Estes Park, Colorado. That place was magical. It was there that I learned to love myself more. I met some amazing people and felt comfortable talking to the guys. I had always been so shy that even looking at a guy was painful.

After my job ended at the Y that summer I went on a three month long NOLS Course (National Outdoor Leadership School) based out of Lander, Wyoming. That was one of the best and more challenging experiences of my life. There were sixteen of us: four girls and twelve young and seemingly immature boys all between the ages of 18 to 24. We backpacked for three weeks in the Wind River Range in Wyoming, rock climbed for two weeks somewhere in Wyoming, went caving for another two weeks, backpacked in Canyonlands in Utah for two weeks and went winter camping in the Snowy River Range, Wyoming for two weeks.

What doesn't kill you makes you stronger. Each time in between sections we would go back to Lander for two days, unpack, shower, get mail and gifts that were sent, make phone calls and eat 'normal' meals. The first day back in Lander was always so fun and the second day I was always a basket case, fearing the anticipation of another new section. Good ole change again...

While I was on NOLS, my parents permanently moved to Vail, Colorado. After NOLS finished in December 1994, I went to Vail, saying to myself, "I am not staying. I will move to Steamboat Springs (another ski town in Colorado north of Vail). I ain't living with my parents."

In December, after I got to Vail, my parents and I took a road trip back to Minnesota to have

Christmas with our family. New Years Day I went to Al's Diner in Dinkytown, located on the University of Minnesota campus, with my college friends Kerrie and Ellen. We must have been having a hangover breakfast. Back then we always used to read our horoscopes. Since it was New Year's Day, the paper had the horoscope for the entire year. Mine said, "You are in or about to become madly enmeshed in love." I knew after my experience on NOLS that something was different. I did feel ready to be in a relationship. Until then, I was so shy my whole life that I never really dated. I moved to Vail as an almost twenty-five year old virgin. I wasn't really "saving myself" for marriage, but there became a time where I knew I wasn't just going to doink anyone.

Regarding my living situation, well, one should never say never. As January 1995 rolled around I decided I would stay in Vail for the rest of the ski season and continued living with my parents. I got a job as a Vail Lift Operator. I began my training that month. There were seventeen of us and I was the only girl. Talk about feeling like a queen! My shyness quickly began to dissolve as I was surrounded by so many fun guys who just wanted to ski and party. I met some of the most amazing people, many of whom I am still close with today.

That spring I was working diligently to make my way back to Estes Park and work a fifth summer at the Y-camp. I applied to become a director of one of the day camps and didn't get it. I was so bummed. As much as I wanted to leave Vail, I decided to stay for the summer and continue to be a Lift Operator. And thank God I didn't get that job at the Y for, as they say, the rest is history.

Meeting the Love of my Life

I met Tom Kiddoo, my husband, while working in Lifts that spring. He was a summer lift mechanics helper. We had our first conversation at the top of the lift house of the Vista Bahn (a former chairlift out of Vail Village which is now Gondola One). I thought he was nice and that he probably had a girlfriend. We talked about his Vasque hiking boots, as I wanted the same pair he was wearing.

As that spring rolled on, I went back to Minnesota for a few weeks in the off-season (May) after the mountain closed. When I got back from Minnesota a bunch of my friends and I went out for the summer's first FAC (Friday Afternoon Club) at Garton's. I ran into Tom there and we had friends in common so we all went over to Nick's, a dingy underground dance bar off of Bridge Street in Vail Village.

At this point we were all loaded. I was watching Tom on the dance floor, dancing like a total jackass, flirting with all of the girls, thinking what a frat boy he was. Next thing I knew he pulled me out on the dance floor and literally stuck his tongue down my throat while attempting to kiss me. I almost died. It was the worst, sloppiest kiss I had ever experienced. The night went on and I ended up driving Tom home. NO, I should not have been driving. I stopped the car in the middle of the road outside his house in West Vail and he told me his sob story of some girl at camp who had broken his heart. I had no idea why he was telling me that.

As Monday morning rolled around I was freaked out about going back to work and seeing Tom. Any other guy I had ever made out with was always a complete douche bag who would ignore me, blow me off, etc afterward. When I first saw Tom at work on Monday, he said, "Haaay, how's it going?" I thought this guy was different and I liked how he greeted me, but I really wasn't interested.

Later in the day a coworker and I had to get

something from the top of the Vista Bahn. I stayed in the work truck while my coworker ran in to grab something. While I was waiting in the car, Tom poked out of the lift house (the bubble barn actually--for those of you who knew old Vail), put his hands on his hips, and made smoochy sounds and motions with his mouth and lips. I about died. I definitely thought this guy was different. I still said to myself I was not interested.

FAC rolled around the next Friday and Tom and I did the same thing--got drunk, smooched at Nick's and again I drove him home. Not proud of the drunk driving. The next day I was operating the Vista Bahn and Tom called me from the bakery he was working at and asked me if I wanted to go to a movie that night. I said yes. We went to see Bridges of Madison County--a great movie and a horrible movie for a first date. I cried the whole time, it was so awkward. After the movie Tom drove me home and just said good night. Since there was no alcohol on board there was no smooching. I was so confused.

I went to meet an old friend in Denver the Monday following and told her about meeting Tom. Saying that I wasn't really interested in Tom and yet I was. When I got back from Denver my mom had left me a note that Tom called at 8:50 pm just to say hello. Tom and I clicked from that point on. We went backpacking in mid June, shortly after we met. It rained the entire time and we had a blast. We literally chatted and played cards in the tent the whole time. Maybe some smooching, definitely no sex yet. I knew after that backpacking trip that Tom was 'the one.'

I felt so comfortable around and with Tom. He was so easy to talk to and I could tell him anything. I told him everything about my past mental health issues: all of the stories. I told him I was on medication and all of the other medications that I had taken over the years. There wasn't anything that I held back from him. It was so nice to be with someone who didn't judge me and accepted me fully.

We did lots of camping and backpacking that summer we met and eventually during one of those backpacking trips we decided to doink and my virginity was out the window. We moved in together over a year after we met in the fall of 1996, got our first dog, Cayman, in early 1997, got engaged in June of 1998, and got married August 1999.

We worked on Lift Operations, Guest Services, and Vail Ski Patrol together. In the spring of 2000 I started my own gardening business, Bedwetters. It was a great complement to working the winters as a ski patroller.

The Quest to Have Children

Virtually since the first day Tom and I met we talked about wanting to have kids. As badly as I wanted to have kids, I was also terrified of having to go off of Tegretol before getting pregnant. I was so worried about becoming depressed and being hospitalized again that it was almost crippling. The biggest concern with pregnancy and Tegretol is the increased risk of neural tube defects. As scared as I was to go off of Tegretol, I did not want to take any risks that could potentially harm the baby.

I began the search for a new shrink in Vail. I found Dr. Johnson who, at the time, worked for Colorado West, which is now Mind Springs Health (an outpatient mental health clinic located in Vail and in Eagle). He was no Dr. Channing, but he was just fine. My biggest concern was being able to go off Tegretol safely. He assured me that he would be able to help me and that I would be closely monitored. I never wanted to go back to where I was when I was hospitalized--so out of control, so scary.

February of 2002 is when I started weaning off Tegretol. I can't remember how long it took--I think about a month. I reduced drinking to almost nothing. I remember feeling the terrible what-ifs. What if I don't get pregnant by the fall? Fall was a horrible time for me. What would I do if the fall rolled around and I wasn't pregnant and I wasn't on medication??? Oh the worry! It was all consuming.

Fortunately there was an angel looking over me. We tried for three months. I found out that I was pregnant May 18th. My pregnancy was amazing. My moods were stable the whole time (although Tom may beg to differ). During my pregnancy I swam three times a week with the masters swim program at the Avon Recreation Center. I dabbled in a little yoga by doing some prenatal VCR tapes at home. I felt great! And I felt very blessed. I was so grateful.

We moved into a new house in Eagle-Vail,

Colorado (a town five miles west of Vail) when I was eight months pregnant and I did great. Remember I always said change was so hard? I was so busy unpacking and organizing that I didn't have time to be in a funk. The greatest thing about moving and being eight months pregnant is that I didn't have to lift a single box. My mom came over a lot in the month before the baby was born to help me unpack the kitchen and hang pictures on the wall. The house was completely ready for a new baby.

I continued running my gardening business while pregnant. I worked at the Lionshead Pass Office (Lionshead is one of Vail Mountain's base areas) right up until the baby was born since I couldn't do ski patrol while being so pregnant.

Miracles

Monday, January 20th (Martin Luther King Day), 2003 at 9:52 pm, Charles (Charlie) Thomas Kiddoo was born. I had a c-section as labor wasn't progressing, his head was stuck and his heart rate was dropping. I was in the hospital for four nights.

When my milk started coming in I was so emotional. I could feel the hormones running through my body and mentally I felt like a train wreck. Between all of the drugs I was on from the c-section and being sleep deprived, I was beside myself. I was thrilled to have this little man and yet so worried about my mental health and of course this new big change.

We got home on Friday, January 24th and I remember my house feeling so weird when we got home. I didn't know which end was up. My mom had made us a meal, thank God. It was challenging trying to get used to the breastfeeding schedule. Charlie would putz around while he was eating so it would take forever. Looking back I think it would have been easier for me to bottle feed him, but I was determined to breastfeed.

Dealing with unknowns and uncertainty made motherhood challenging--it still does at times! Not knowing when he was going to need to eat, not knowing when he was going to wake up definitely created anxiety for me. Charlie 'slept' in our room for the first two weeks after he was born. I didn't sleep though. I could hear every little movement and snort that he made and I would lie awake in anticipation of him needing to eat.

When we went to see our family doctor for our two week checkup I was delirious, so tired. She told us to move Charlie into his own room so that I could sleep better. Moving him into his crib in his room made a world of difference. I remember she told me I wouldn't make a good doctor because I needed my sleep. So true. When I don't get enough sleep I am a basket case. So it seems.

Time flew along after having little Charlie. Fortunately he was a really good baby and learned to sleep through the night at eight weeks old. What a blessing that was.

Fast forward two and a half years later to Labor Day, September 5th, 2005, when we had a baby girl, Catie (or, as Charlie called her in utero, Baby Dragon). I am not sure what the significance, if any, of having two children born on holidays means. All I know is that having two children, one of each, a boy and a girl is all I ever wanted. After all of the mental health stuff I had gone through and being on medication for so long, I was never sure that having kids was possible. I had always hoped and never lost sight of that hope. I had clung on to Dr. Marshall's words that "someday Julie will have children."

Having a 2 year old and a newborn was work, as anyone who has raised children can attest to. Tom was a bond trader at the time, so he would leave for work at 8 pm after the kids went to bed and would come home by 7 am the next morning. He would 'sleep' through much of the day. Trying to keep a 2 year old, a newborn, and a dog who would bark every time the wind blew, quiet was interesting to say the least. Fortunately my sister-in-law, Martha, had kids the same age and her husband, Kurt, was bond trading too so having Martha was a huge support. We did everything together from running with the four kids in the joggers, to taking the 2 year olds skating, to drinking beer and hanging out together. Thank God for that support.

My mental health over the course of being pregnant and having these two babies was pretty stable. I was extremely blessed that I was able to go off of my medication to be able to have these children. I definitely felt as though I had a guardian angel looking over me.

Two Steps Forward, One Step Back

Shortly after the beginning of 2007, Tom's bond trading career came to end. That was an extremely difficult time. It's hard to explain but trading is very emotional. Tom wasn't making any money doing it--as a matter of fact he was just losing money, the bond trading firm's money.

We had lived off of our savings for the two years while he was trading and the time had come for trading to end. With that change came the change of Tom sleeping at night and us sharing a bed again. Sometime over the course of trading, Tom had developed sleep apnea. His snoring was awful! I would lie awake at night and couldn't sleep because the snoring was so bad. As mentioned before, I can get beside myself when I don't get enough sleep.

While all of this was happening I also got my first sinus infection. I went to the doctor and got a Z-pack for my sinus infection and was given Ambien to help me sleep. The Ambien worked for one night and after that it had the opposite effect. My sleep got worse and worse and my mental health was quickly going down the tubes. I was so anxious I thought I was going to crawl out of my skin and I also felt depressed. That old familiar feeling of depression and anxiety was creeping back in. I knew that something wasn't right and I knew that I needed help as soon as possible to turn myself around.

I went to our family doctor and told her about my moods and sleep and she suggested taking a drug called Neurontin or Gabapentin (generic). She said it would help regulate my sleep and I would most likely only need to be on it for a short amount of time. She wanted me to consult Dr. Johnson to see if he agreed with me taking this medication. She also suggested that Tom sleep in a separate bedroom for at least a couple of weeks so that I could get my sleep back in order. She said it had taken me a bit to get in the funk that I was in, so it was probably going to take a bit for me to get out of the funk. In some ways that was helpful to not rush the process and in other ways hearing that sucked as I wanted to get better as soon as possible.

I went to Dr. Johnson and he agreed with our family doctor that taking Neurontin would be a good choice. We worked with my dosage over time. He said that Neurontin not only regulates sleep, it is also a mood stabilizer and works on physical pain. I felt pretty good taking Neurontin knowing that it helped to regulate sleep, but was not so thrilled that it was a mood stabilizer. I felt as though I was creeping back into old patterns. I felt defeated to be going back on a medication--how did I make it five years without being on anything, especially with two pregnancies and two postpartum periods? And yet I knew being on a medication was the one thing that could pull me out of the funk that I was in. I knew medication had helped me in the past and I just wanted to feel better. Feeling better mentally meant more to me than suffering and being medication free.

Tom ended up moving to our downstairs guest bedroom. It was meant to be for a couple of weeks and it ended up being for two years. I was so anxious going to bed that the thought of having him next to me and snoring seemed unbearable.

The Neurontin worked for me to a certain point. I was able to sleep while I was on it for the most part and it pulled me out of the funk that I was in, but after a period of time I don't think it was really doing anything for me. I had a love-hate relationship with Neurontin. I was glad that I had found a medication that helped to regulate my sleep and my mood with no side effects; however, I resisted being on any medication. It wasn't so much the being on the medication that bothered me; it was the fear I had of "what if." What if I forgot my pills when I went out of town? What would happen to me? There were nights where I would forget to take them and I could barely sleep a wink. I would lie awake anxious for hours only to have the light bulb go on of 'oh duh, I forgot to take Neurontin before I went to bed.' Neurontin is a drug that has to be weaned off of gradually over time. Going off cold turkey is not safe as it can cause anxiety, difficulty sleeping, nausea, pain, and sweating and who knows what else.

The other "what if" fear I had was what would I be like without being on medication? Did I need to depend on something for the rest of my life? It wasn't really the stigma of being on a medication I had an issue with, it was more of a fear of who I would be or how I would feel without being on a medication? What if I forgot my pills and I couldn't sleep and then who would I be without good sleep? I'd probably be strung out and end up back in the hospital or something like that. Fear, fear, fear.

After some time of being on Neurontin I felt like myself again. Tom was still sleeping in the guest bedroom and that drove me crazy. Being married, I felt that a married couple ought to share a bed. It felt so weird that Tom was in a separate bedroom from me and what felt even worse was all of the fear I had surrounding the 'what if's.' What if Tom did sleep in the same bed as me, would his snoring keep me awake all night? And then what? I can't imagine how Tom felt sleeping in a different bedroom. I never asked him at the time. He was so amazing and was willing to do anything to have me happy and healthy.

Discovering Yoga

My dear friend, Rachel DeLong, had been a rock for me during the process of Tom ending the bond trading and my whole sleep issue, etc. She kept saying to me, "Julie, I have a card for a free week of yoga at the Vail Athletic Club for you." I kept saying that I didn't have time. At one point I told her that I didn't have enough time to go and that I was too stressed out to go. Someone overheard me saying that and said, "Well that is probably a reason for you to go." I still wasn't ready to hit the yoga mat yet. As a matter of fact, a year prior, I was handed a week free card at the end of a snowshoe race in Beaver Creek by Kelly Heath, who later become my very first yoga teacher.

In March of 2007 we found out that Tom's amazing dad, also named Tom Kiddoo, Jr. (my Tom is the III) was diagnosed with a rare blood disorder called Myelofibrosis. It is a blood disease similar to Leukemia. Tom, Jr. had to had to have blood transfusions bi-monthly. By the fall of 2007 he was told he needed to have a bone marrow transplant. We were told that the transplant would add two more years to his life. Unfortunately Tom passed away October 24, 2007, a month after being told he needed a bone marrow transplant. He never got the chance to have the transplant. That same month I also lost a dear friend and gardening client. Needless to say it was a tough month.

It was so sad losing my father-in-law and even sadder to watch Tom in so much pain from losing his dad. It was a rough go for a while. 2007 felt like a year of hell. So many things were going on around me that I truly had no control over and yet I took it all on and I was a basket case. Rachel DeLong was persistent in asking me to go to yoga. My answer was always no, until a week after Tom, Jr. died, when I finally said yes. Despite all that was going on around me I knew that ultimately I was the only one who had the power to change my life. I was the only one who had control over my thoughts and mind and I knew that it was time to make a change.

I went with Rachel to my first yoga class at the Vail Athletic Club Tuesday November 6th, 2007. This was my first Baptiste Yoga class ever. Kelly Heath was the teacher. I will never forget this day. There were mirrors all over the room and despite not loving seeing myself in the mirror I knew that something was different. Kelly spoke of gratitude during class and I felt as though she was talking directly to me. She played Amazing Grace in savasana (the final resting pose of the class). I was so grateful I had a towel to cover my eyes so that no one could see me crying. I was able to be sad about Tom's dad on my mat. I was able to let all of my emotions out at the time they came up. After class I felt amazing.

That same week I went to two more classes, one with Jessa Munion and one with Rachel Nelson. They, too, were Baptiste teachers. I couldn't put my finger on it, but something was different about this yoga. I felt that each teacher was speaking directly to me in class and that they all had something so special to share.

After my first week of free yoga I bought a punch-card at The Vail Athletic Club. I continued to go two to three times a week. I was hooked. I felt great every time I went to class, physically and mentally. The yoga was challenging and each time I tried a new pose and 'got it' I could take the parallels from the lessons I learned on my mat and apply them to everyday life. Baron Baptiste (the founder of Baptiste Yoga), says "Wherever you go there you are" and "Your mat is a reflection of you." If you're putting in the effort on your mat, you will get results off your mat. Conversely if you are not putting in the effort on your mat, those results (or lack thereof) will show up everywhere.

The Healing Begins

In the fall of 2007, shortly after I started doing yoga, I went to a now deceased healer, Cathy Zeeb, who had a PhD in Metaphysics, was an Ordained Minister, a Reiki Master, and a Certified Addictions Psychotherapist. She could also read and see auras and chakras (energy centers). I was done with shrinks. I wanted something new. At the first appointment I had with her I told her the history of my mental health. When I was finished she said, "Okay I'm looking at you and I heard all of what you were saying. And something happened to you when you were 7." I completely left out the part where I was molested, as though it never happened.

She didn't know what it was that happened when I was 7 but she could tell there was a trauma there as she could see stuck energy in my second chakra (the energy center located in between the pubic bone and the belly button). So I told her the entire story. She went on to tell me that when things happen to us and we do not release them they can manifest into depression. She said that once we change our thoughts about what happened we can release what happened from our bodies. I thought she was crazy when she said we can change our thoughts. My thoughts owned me at the time. I had no idea what she was talking about.

That was the first time I started to see that what happened to me when I was 7 could have possibly triggered my mental health issues. I know now without a shadow of doubt in my mind that being molested and keeping it a secret for ten years is one of the reasons why my depression became so severe. The attack when I was 16 also contributed to the depression.

http://www.heretohelp.bc.ca/factsheet/childhood-sexual-abuse-a-mental-health-issue

Mental illness—Experiencing childhood sexual abuse does not mean that you will develop a mental illness, but it is one of many risk factors. People who experience childhood sexual abuse may have a higher risk of experiencing anxiety disorders (such as post-traumatic stress disorder),15 depression,16 eating disorders,16 dissociative disorders17 and personality disorders18.

(Footnote numbers refer to publications mentioned in the original article)

In Brene Brown's book, *Daring Greatly*, she quotes a book by James Pennebaker on page 82, "You're only as sick as your secrets. In a pioneering study, psychologist James Pennebaker and his colleagues studied what happened when trauma survivors-specifically rape and incest survivors-kept their experiences secret. The research found that the act of not discussing a traumatic event or confiding it to another person could be more damaging than the actual event. Conversely, when people shared their stories and experiences, their physical health improved, their doctor's visits decreased, and they showed significant decreases in their stress hormones."

Brene goes on to say, "Since his early

work on the effect of secret keeping, Pennebaker has focused much of his research on the healing power of expressive writing. In his book Writing to Heal, Pennebaker writes, "since the mid-1980s an increasing number of studies have focused on the value of expressive writing as a way to bring about healing. The evidence is mounting that the act of writing as little as fifteen or twenty minutes a day for three or four days can produce measurable changes in physical and mental health. Emotional writing can also affect people's sleep habits, work efficiency, and how they connect with others"."

After rereading that part of Brene's book and then typing the content into this book, I see how keeping the molestation a secret for ten years did a significant amount of damage to my soul-body, mind and spirit. And although I wasn't walking around with a consciousness of what happened to me, my body kept score for me.

Since that time I have done a number of

things to heal that experience. I have gotten clear over the years that because of what had happened to me I had been carrying around a huge cloak of victimhood. Many places I would go or interactions I would have I would go into a place of 'poor me.' "Why are they being so mean to me? So and so is such a bully. Life's not fair. Why me?" Even though I was molested when I was 7 I was carrying on as though it was still happening in the present moment. I started to see the impact of what had happened and the way of being I had adopted from these experiences.

Personal Revolution

In January of 2008, shortly after I started yoga, I signed up for my first 40 Days to Personal Revolution program (a Baptiste self-development program) led by Kelly Heath at The Vail Athletic Club. It was actually 42 days, since Kelly added on an extra two days to make it an even six weeks. This program blew my doors off. 40 days is essentially a six week program of yoga, meditation, mindful eating and journaling. Since 2008 I have done, assisted or led over twenty of these programs and each time I have participated in one I have gotten amazing results and something different each time.

Initially when I did my first 40 Days program, I was only interested in doing more yoga and deepening my practice. I had no desire to change my eating habits and I definitely had the judgment that people who meditated were weird. However, being that I tend to lean toward being a perfectionist, I decided to take on the program seriously so that I could get access to what the program results boasted.

During the program I did tons of yoga, meditated twice a day, did my first cleanse, conquered fears that I never knew I had, lost weight and felt great. Once the program was over I continued to meditate for fifteen minutes each morning. After the second 40 days program I meditated twice a day regularly. I knew that if I meditated at the beginning of the day it gave my day a fresh, clean start and if I meditated at the end of the day it helped me sleep better.

My diet also changed even though at the beginning of the program I was completely resistant to changing what I ate. My mid-morning snack used to used be a Morningstar Farms meatless sausage patty. I would throw it in the microwave for forty-two seconds, wrap a paper towel around it, put it in a snack-sized Ziplock bag, stuff it into my purse and away I went. Somewhere during that first 40 days that sausage patty snack shifted to a sliced up apple, which is still my mid-morning snack now.

The results that I received from doing that first 40 days program were unbelievable. In addition to doing more yoga than I had ever, beginning a new meditation practice and mindful eating, my fear of change seemed to lessen. It was in the 40 Days program that I began to trust in something bigger than myself and learned that I didn't have to fear change as much as I had previously. I learned that things always have a way of working out and to trust the process.

Becoming a Yoga Teacher

During the summer of 2008 a little birdie popped into my head saying, "What if you became a yoga teacher?" I was an early childhood education major. I always had a passion for teaching. When I was on ski patrol I taught CPR and First-Aid to the incoming rookies and to the Community Guest Service people. I was so passionate about teaching people who were genuinely interested in what I was teaching.

In August of 2008 I had coffee with Jessa Munion and I told her that I was interested in teaching yoga. Jessa told me to look at Baron Baptiste's website to learn more information about his Level One teacher training that was going to take place the following February on the Big Island of Hawaii. My first response in my head when she told me to look into this was, 'There is no way I can do this. There's no way I can leave my kids (at that time they were three and five) and there is no way I can afford the program.' With that resistance acknowledged, I looked at the website anyway.

The following Monday I went to Rachel Nelson's class and she said, "Oh my gosh, I hear you want to go to Level One. That's awesome. Just do it." I was so embarrassed. I forgot to tell Jessa that I didn't want anyone to know I was thinking about teaching yoga. I didn't want anyone to look at me differently. And now that I teach yoga, I totally get where Jessa and Rachel were coming from in their enthusiasm to send me off to a teacher training with Baron. I ran into Jessa early September of that year and I told her that I had looked into Baron's website. I told her that it was a lot of money to spend. What she said in response was the best, "Just look at this as an investment in yourself, your life, your family and your future." She got me to see past my own resistance and got me in touch with what I truly wanted.

There is something so special about Baptiste Yoga. It's real. It's physical. It touches people's hearts. It certainly had touched mine and I was ready for more. Even though I wasn't 100% certain I wanted to teach yoga after Level One, I knew that it was a means to an end. I wanted more personal growth. I wanted to be able to share with others what I had gotten from yoga. It was time to pay it forward. So I signed up for Level One.

February 2009 I headed on a plane to the Big Island of Hawaii to do Level One with Baron Baptiste. I had no idea what to expect. At the time the Level One teacher trainings were called Boot Camps. I did have an idea that it was going to be challenging and intense. My teachers, Kelly, Rachel and Jessa, didn't say a lot about Level One, but I heard enough from them to know it was possibly going to kick my ass.

Kick my ass it did. Level One was a week long intense teacher training. Yes, I learned how to teach yoga from this training and really,

I learned and discovered so much more. The days were long. There were some nights we didn't get to bed until 2:00 am and then we had to be ready to go the next day by 7:00 am. I was completely out of my comfort zone. I had to let go of control, resistance, and the outcome and just go where the training led me.

Before I went to Level One, every night at 10:00 pm before I went to bed I had a snack that consisted of four Deli Style Rye Triscuits with one slice of Swiss cheese evenly divided among the four crackers. I had created this whole story that if I didn't have that food before I went to bed, I wouldn't be able to sleep. Since Triscuits and Swiss cheese weren't available at Level One I had to give up that snack. By the time I got home that habit was gone.

Toward the end of the training we did this exercise where we wrote a story about something that had happened to us in the past and that was still causing us suffering. I wrote all about my past with depression and all of my fears and concerns about my sleep and that Tom wasn't sleeping in the same bedroom as me. That whole situation really bothered me.

While we were writing Baron told us to watch for what was real and what was stuff that we had made up. Once we finished writing (I wrote seven pages in my journal) we grabbed a partner and had to read our story over and over again. The exercise was to cross off the things that weren't real--the subjective stuff that was just made up. We had to keep reading our story over and over again until we felt like our story didn't have any charge for us. And we were to continue crossing off things that weren't real and only stick to the facts. Baron would ask the people who were complete to raise their hands and for those of us who weren't complete to switch partners. I was one of the last people to get complete.

Out of that seven page paper the only fact that was on that paper was that Tom was sleeping in a different bedroom. That was it. All of the other stuff was attachment to suffering that had happened in the past that I was still carrying around like a medal. I was living in a victim world.

I'll never forget talking to Tom from the Honolulu airport on the way home from Level One and saying to him, "Tom, when I get home I don't want you to go back downstairs. I want you to stay in our bedroom." I think he about died and was probably wondering what the hell had happened to me over the past seven days.

I am happy and proud to say that since I have been back from Level One in 2009 Tom and I have been sleeping in the same bed. I never thought it was going to be possible to shift through all of the fears and anxiety I had about my sleep. Level One gave me access to a whole new way of being with sleep and my relationship with myself among many other amazing breakthroughs and transformations.

As I said, before I went to Level One, I wasn't even sure if I wanted to teach yoga. After Level 1, I knew I wanted to teach yoga. April 11, 2009 I taught my first yoga class at the Vail Athletic Club. I can still picture the six people who were in the class. I was so nervous. The night before I taught I must have written six pages in my journal of what I was going to say while I was teaching. I had been reading an article titled, "*Spring Clean Your Closets, Spring Clean Your Life.*" Yep--that was the message I was going to bring home while I was teaching. At some point while I was journaling I came to my senses. I scrapped all my writings, said, "fuck it" and just taught yoga.

I survived teaching my first class. It was my second class where I thought I was going to die. I knew Jessa was going to be attending my class to give me feedback. While I was driving up I-70 on the way to the Vail Athletic Club I thought I was going to puke. I wanted to turn my car around and head home. When I got to the front doors of the club I held the handle of the front door and said, "I can't do this. I should just go home." And a bigger voice inside my head said, "Yes, you are going to do this. Go get in there." And I did and I was horrified the whole time.

After class Jessa gave me great feedback and also asked me if I even liked teaching yoga. I guess I was so nervous it came off as though I didn't like teaching. I suppose I didn't really like it that day and yet I knew there was something out there bigger than me that was calling me to teach and to give back to people what I had received over the short amount of time I had been doing yoga.

I continued teaching at the Vail Athletic Club and did two 40 Days programs a year, in January and July.

Face to Face with Depression

By January 2010 I applied for Baptiste Yoga's Level Two Teacher Training which took place in May of that year. One of the questions on the application (which is probably on most applications) asked if I was taking any medications and if I was under the supervision of a doctor. I always hated answering that question. I felt a lot of shame around being on a medication. I never knew if I should tell the truth when filling out the applications or lie.

Since it was a Baptiste program and a huge essence of the work is living in your truth, I decided to be truthful when filling out the application. About a week after I applied to Level Two I received a phone call from Baptiste Yoga saying that they had gotten my application and that they needed to have a letter of approval from my psychiatrist before I got accepted to the training.

I will never forget how I reacted that day when

I got that phone call from Baptiste Yoga. I was so pissed off. I was feeling sorry for myself. I was being a victim. I was mad that I had to go through those steps to prove that I was okay. I felt judged (even though I wasn't being judged). I was telling myself a bunch of crazy stories about myself, none of which were true and I suppose they were what I believed about myself at the time.

I called my shrink and got the necessary paperwork filled out for Baptiste Yoga. And I understood where Baptiste was coming from. They want to make sure the participants are going to be safe and healthy during the trainings as they can be quite intense physically and emotionally. My reactions had nothing to do with Baptiste or the paperwork, and everything to do with my lack of acceptance of my mental health.

January 2010, the same month I applied for Level Two, I had the privilege of working with my "healer," TeriLeigh, a woman whom I credit so much for where I am today with my well being. Just a little background on TeriLeigh as she is many things. She went through a major depression when she was younger, she was formerly a certified Baptiste yoga teacher, she sees auras and can read people's chakras (energy centers in the body). She holds one hour sessions with people, either in person or remotely, and listens to what the person says. She has a great way of making sense of whatever it is that one is going through and offers a clear perspective. She shares what she sees and hears and offers "prescriptions" for healing--not drug ones.

Initially I had been feeling resistant to seeing TeriLeigh. She was in Vail teaching yoga and offering her sessions the summer prior and I thought the whole thing seemed 'weird' to say the least: distinctly different from all the shrinks I had seen in the past. I attended a few of TeriLeigh's classes while she was out in January 2010. At the end of one of her classes she shared her story of her depression. Even though

I had heard it the summer prior, this time when I heard I was ready to listen. Something grabbed my heart and I was ready for a change, so I set up an appointment with TeriLeigh. I knew that I had been fighting accepting depression and it was time to try on something new.

While in the session with TeriLeigh I told her my whole story of depression and anxiety. I told her about applying for Level Two and having to get a medical release from my shrink and how triggered I had gotten. She listened to the whole thing and when I was finished talking she said, "When I see people who have depression I see an animal-like monster. With you I see an animal-like monster over your left shoulder. He's not mean, he's sweet looking like Animal from the Muppets."

She also told me that when I was catatonic I went to the spirit world and I downloaded information from the spirit world that no one else has access to. The whole time I was hearing these things I kept reminding myself to be open minded. These were words I had never heard from any shrink.

TeriLeigh went on to say that the monster was actually a good thing. That he was hosting off of me. If we killed him we would kill the host--me. TeriLeigh asked me about the medication that I was on. Did it have any side effects? It had none, except I took a nap everyday. She said naps were really good for me and that every time I napped I downloaded more messages from the spirit world. She said, "If you don't feel any side effects and it's working why would you need to go off of it?" These were just the words that I needed to hear at the time.

I told her that I felt pressure from society to go off of medication. She said, "Well society is fucked up." I told her I felt pressure from the yoga world to go off medication. She said, "The yoga world is fucked up. Julie, it is your mission in life to go out and share your stories and to break down the stigma that people have toward depression and medication.

This is your purpose in life."

At this point my wheels were turning. I had never heard this perspective before. TeriLeigh was getting me to shift from resenting my depression to accepting, embracing and loving it. I asked her how I was able to go through five years without being on a medication. Five years where in that time I had two pregnancies and two postpartums. How was I fine during that time? She said that I was meant to have my children and that the universe/God was doing everything in its power to make sure that I had those two babies. There was some protective power over me making sure that everything was going to be okay. She said that I could be on the medication for the rest of my life.

I left my session with TeriLeigh literally feeling ten pounds lighter, mentally and physically. I felt such a sense of acceptance of my mental health. I had been judging myself and making myself wrong for years for what I had gone through. I had so much shame around everything. I would only tell people about my past with depression if I knew them really well and trusted them. The whole thing was such a secret. If I did tell people about my past I would make them swear that they wouldn't tell a soul. And now I had TeriLeigh telling me that it was my mission in life to go out into the world and share of myself so that I could help others who struggle with anxiety and depression.

The coolest thing about TeriLeigh is that she has such an awesome way of making sense of everything. She is a conduit and receives information from her spirit guides when leading sessions. She is never suggestive, only offers clarity in a way that completely makes sense. She is so relatable. I have watched the transformation in others with whom she has worked. I would not be where I am today without the work I have done with TeriLeigh.

Sharing the Journey

The next evening after meeting with TeriLeigh I attended my 40 Days meeting. It was the first time I had ever shared my story with an entire group of people. Talk about letting my spiritual balls hang out! I even told the group that I was labeled Bipolar in high school. I will never forget what happened after sharing all that I did. Just as soon as I finished sharing, the sky lit up and fireworks went off on Vail Mountain. I know there was some event happening on the mountain and the timing could not have been any more perfect. I felt as though I had been completely acknowledged for sharing. It was a sign for me that I was on the right path. The time of keeping everything a secret was over. It was time for Julie to come out, to stop hiding and to start living--not only for me, for those who need me to be me so that they can be them.

I saw my new shrink, Dr. Reichert (Dr.

Johnson was transferred to a different office), the following week and told him about my session with TeriLeigh. I was worried about telling him that I had gone to an 'alternative' form of therapy: I was almost apologetic. I was pleasantly surprised with his reaction when I told him that I had seen TeriLeigh. He said, "You have to have a balance between Western and Eastern medicine." That was a relief to hear. I told him that TeriLeigh said that I could be on my medication for the rest of my life. Ironically Dr. Reichert said, "Well, Julie, you certainly don't have to be. If there comes a time when or if you want to go off of Neurontin, we can certainly help you wean off of it." I wanted to hear nothing of the sort at the time. TeriLeigh had just given me permission to be on the medication and to accept it. I was happy being just where I was. At least for the time being.

2010 rolled along. I went to Baptiste Yoga's Level Two with Baron in May. As with all the Baptiste programs, I got many incredible insights, and had meaningful breakdowns and breakthroughs. I continued to teach yoga at The Vail Athletic Club.

The fall of 2010 brought a lot of sadness. We lost our almost fourteen year old Golden Retriever, Cayman, in September. My mom had open heart surgery the same month to have her aortic valve replaced. Thank God that surgery went really well--it was very scary though before she had it.

The day after Thanksgiving that year our five year old nephew, Max Krieg, was rushed to a hospital in Reno (from Truckee, California). He had croup and his throat had closed up and he stopped breathing. The paramedics did everything they could to keep Max alive on the ambulance drive to Reno. There were times at the hospital where hope would enter, but in the end Max couldn't be saved and sadly he left this world on December 2nd, 2010. Max was the same age as my daughter, Catie. They were born thirteen days apart. Watching my sister in law, Martha, and her husband, Kurt, go through this devastating time was beyond painful.

While Max was in the hospital and we knew things weren't looking good, Tom flew out to Reno to be with Martha and the family. I drove him to the airport. When I got back from the airport that same night my house was empty. The kids were at my parent's place for the night and there was no dog there to greet me. My house felt lonely and creepy. I was taking phone calls from concerned relatives. I got in the tub that night feeling scared and sad and wondering/worrying how losing Max would affect my mental health.

While I was in the tub I got the most unusual sensation for me. It was this incredible sense of calm and trust. I knew in my heart that no matter what happened with Max, no matter how devastating losing him was going to be, I knew in my heart of hearts that I was going to be okay. The Yogis call this *Santosha* or contentment: the knowledge that no matter what happens I will be OK. *Santosha* is one of the practices of the *Niyamas* or observances, one of the eight limbs of yoga. Although I knew that losing Max had nothing to do with me, I knew how easily affected by outside circumstances I could become and this gift of *Santosha* helped me through this hard time.

The next two years my life changed direction dramatically. An opportunity came along to manage a new yoga studio and then somewhere along the way I decided I wanted to own a yoga studio rather than just manage one. Being around my Baptiste family always got me so lit up and inspired by all of the people. They always seemed like they had it all together. I wanted to be one of them. Together with my new business partner and good friend, Rachel Nelson, we pursued our common dream and opened the doors to Revolution Power Yoga on January 18th, 2012. Owning a yoga studio has been one of the most challenging and rewarding things that I have ever done. I love being a stand for community and others' growth. Being witness to other people's transformation has been so inspiring and mind blowing.

Once we had the studio up and running, I decided it was time to start sharing the tools I had learned from yoga to offer healing to others. As I already mentioned, in my first session with TeriLeigh she said, "Julie, it is your mission in life to go out and share your stories and to break down and demystify the stigma that people have toward depression and medication. This is your purpose in life." Therefore, in the fall of 2012 I created a workshop 'Yoga for the Big D: Transform Anxiety and Depression through Yoga.' The first two hour workshop I led was packed. It felt like such a rite of passage for me to finally be able to share my story with everyone so that I could offer healing to others. It was amazing.

The following spring I led a four week Yoga for the Big D series and was completely out of my league. Some of the women in the group were dealing with things that were beyond my level of expertise to handle, despite what my personal mental health experiences were. I think I approached leading this series as though it was going to be the be all and end all and that everyone in the workshop was going to be healed. Fortunately I was working with a therapist who assisted me with this workshop. My mom also said, "Julie, think of your own path. It wasn't just one thing that got you better. It has been many things that have helped you. What you are offering these women is just one piece of the pie." Hearing that took so much pressure off of me. I had put so much pressure on myself thinking that if these women in the workshop didn't get everything out of it then it was a reflection of me.

While I was leading the four week series I had decided that it would be a good idea to attend a training to give me more tools and also training credibility, along with me having my own personal experiences with anxiety and depression. So I applied to attend the LifeForce Yoga training with

Amy Weintraub. That was an incredible decision. (More on this in the *A World of Possibility* chapter.) I knew that I wanted to help people who struggle with depression and I didn't want to feel like I was in over my head again.

Healing the Past

In December of 2012 I attended Level Three teacher training with Baron in Tulum, Mexico. While I was at the training we did an exercise called Emptying Out. The intention is to 'empty out' any stuckness that one may have. One of the questions in the exercise is "What happened that should not have happened?" Being molested by Paul is what kept coming up for me and I was so surprised as this was not something I consciously thought about ever. When I got home from Level Three I was still churning about being molested and the impact it had on me.

I knew it was time to really put the past behind me, so that's when I contacted TeriLeigh. After I shared about being molested TeriLeigh told me to write a letter of all that had happened. "Get everything out on paper. All the feelings, anger, sadness, etc. Get everything down. Then after you write the letter, burn it and save the ashes." That was step one. "The next thing you'll do is buy an animal heart of some sort." At this point my heart rate started to speed up and I was telling myself this woman is whacked, crazy, completely out of her mind. And yet I knew I wanted to move forward from where I was so I continued to listen to what she was asking me to do. "It can be from a chicken, or a cow. You can go to the butchers at the grocery store and see what they have." "Okay," I said. And the instructions went on. "Once you have the heart you will find some jewels, perhaps something from what one of your kids made to represent something happy and joyful." At this point I'm thinking this is really fucked up. She wants me to do what with WHAT??? And I continued to listen. "Then you put something in the heart that represents Yoga for the Big D. Once you have those things in the heart, you'll wrap the heart in gauze. The gauze represents the bandage to heal the wound. Then you'll dig a hole, put the heart in the hole, sprinkle the letter on top of the heart and bury it. When you plant things they become fertilizer for something new." At this point she definitely had my attention and I was wondering how in the hell I was ever going to pull this off. Not to mention it was January and there was no way I was going to be able to dig a hole in the ground.

Since I am rather resourceful this is how I executed TeriLeigh's prescription. I wrote the letter and got everything out on paper, burned it in my driveway in the dead of winter in an old Crockpot. Once the letter was fully burned, I scooped up the ashes and put them in a small Ziplock bag and stored them in the garage for a future date when the ground would be thawed.

In the meantime I called local grocery stores asking them if they sold animal hearts. Those were probably some of the most insane phone calls I have ever made. I ended up contacting Cut, an upscale butcher shop in Edwards, Colorado. This is how the phone call went. Me, "Um hi. I am calling to see if you sell animal hearts? Do you have cow hearts specifically?" The guy at Cut, "Um yeah we could probably get you one of those. It'll be about a week. We'll call you when it comes in." "Great, thank you", I said.

About a week later I received a call that my cow heart was ready. When I picked it up the guy at the store asked me if I was going to do an experiment with it. Since I kept being molested a secret for so long I told him the truth. I told him what had happened and what this exercise was meant to do. It felt really good to be so open about it without being dramatic about it. No more secrets.

Since it was the dead of winter, I knew I wasn't going to be able to bury the heart and I knew that I could at least prep the heart for burial and put it in the freezer until the ground thawed in the spring. One thing I want to mention before I continue is that once I started unearthing all of this stuff and how it had impacted my whole life, I shared it with my amazing husband and my children. I knew what the impact of keeping things a secret for so long was and it has been cathartic to share with my family. Not to mention, as far as being molested goes, I wanted my kids to know about that so that they could be prepared in case anyone ever tried to touch them inappropriately. My kids know everything. It was important to me to be open with them and still is.

Once I got the cow heart home, the kids were very curious about seeing it. Our kitchen has a high counter top with two bar stools upon which my kids were perched. I had asked my daughter, who is a perpetual artist, if she had any gems or jewels that could go in the heart. She found a red and a blue flower intended originally for scrap booking. She said the red one represented love and the blue one stood for peace. I had an old flyer from Yoga for the Big D laying around so I cut the title off of it and folded into a minute square. I got out a cookie sheet and laid the heart on that. The heart had been filleted open and was about the size of two flattened footballs laying next to each other. It was also vacuum sealed. I was nervous to take off the wrapping. I have a hard enough time dealing with raw chicken let alone an enormous cow heart. I put on a pair of rubber gloves--no way I was going to make direct skin contact with that heart. As my children anxiously watched I placed the cow heart down on a rimmed cookie sheet. I used scissors to take off the plastic wrap. I used a knife and cut a small slit into the side of the heart and that is where I put the jewels from Catie and the folded Yoga for the Big D piece of paper. Once I had those things in the heart, I folded the heart in half. I wrapped the gauze around the heart. Once that was complete I put Saran Wrap around the heart, put in a Ziplock bag and put in the freezer in our garage to await the day in the spring when the ground thawed. With the completion of each step of this prescription that TeriLeigh had prescribed for me I started to feel lighter.

A few months later the ground had thawed

and it was time to bury the heart. At first I wasn't sure where to bury the heart. I was concerned that, depending on where it got buried, it might get dug up by an animal. TeriLeigh said that was okay because it was more about performing the ritual than actually making sure that the heart stayed buried. So I decided to bury the heart in one of the gardens at my house. Charlie was very curious about this whole process. He stood with me while I dug the hole. And I dug that thing deep--there was no way I wanted to see this thing get dug up. As I was digging the hole, Charlie was asking me questions about what had happened. I was bawling. And not because I was sad, but rather I started to experience freedom. For thirty-six years I had been holding on to all of the trauma of being molested. It was time to let it go. Once the hole was dug I set the heart at the bottom of the hole. I took off the plastic bag and the Saran wrap. Then I took the ashes of the letter I had written, opened the plastic bag and sprinkled the letter on top of the heart. Then I put the dirt back in the hole and the prescription was complete. I can honestly say that the exercise transformed my relationship to what had happened to me when I was 7, as crazy as that whole thing may sound.

I am into animal symbolism and this is what *http://www.whats-your-sign.com/* had to say about the cow:

"In many cultures, animal symbolism of the cow is married to the concept of Mother Earth, and has been a symbol of fertility, nurturing, and power for centuries. This makes udder sense (pardon the pun), cows have been generous with their life force for eons. They are closely associated with provision and very earth-associated in symbolism. The cow is also a lunar symbol, aligning itself with feminine (yin) qualities among the Chinese yin-yang energies. A quick-list of animal symbolism of the cow would include Patience, Nourishment, Abundance, Fertility, Female Power, Potential, Possibility, Calming,

Grounded, Provision, and Beginnings."

I just knew that by burying the cow heart it was going to become fertilizer for something new.

A World of Possibility

I have come to realize that my personal development is a lifelong process. The many programs and courses I have taken have called to me for one reason or another and each has enriched my journey and given me tools that help me to deal with my depression and grow. In January of 2014 I did a week long training with LifeForce Yoga called The LifeForce Yoga Practitioner Training for Depression and Anxiety, Level One. This was a comprehensive training for yoga teachers and therapists where we were taught several techniques to help with anxiety, depression and mood. We learned a variety of things from pranayama (breath work), chakra clearings, yoga nidra (similar to a guided meditation: done lying down, one hour of yoga nidra is equivalent to four hours of sleep. It is highly effective for mood and sleep regulation), Ayurveda (ancient sister science to yoga regarding health and wellness), energizing and calming yoga poses and more.

The tools I have learned have not only aided in maintaining my own mental health; they have also developed my ability to help others in a similar frame of mind. After the training I went through the certification process with LifeForce Yoga to become a LifeForce Yoga Practitioner. As a result, I am able to work with clients on a 1:1 basis that is catered specifically to the individual. I also met Twyla Gingrich through this training. Twyla is a mental health counselor, certified yoga teacher and LifeForce Practitioner and resides in the Vail Valley.

Another personal growth program I can't say enough about is The Landmark Forum. I participated in it during the fall of 2013. It runs over a long weekend, from all day Friday through to Sunday and the following Tuesday night. I was invited to attend it by a friend and fellow yoga teacher, Mariah Schuette, after I had been amazed by seeing her transformation. She invited my friend Amy Archer and myself down to Denver from Vail on the Tuesday night of her program. I sat in the chair that evening and was blown away by the transformation of the individuals I witnessed. So I signed up.

One of the promises of the work at Landmark is about getting complete with your past. If you're not complete with your past, whether it's with another person, a situation or something else, that incompletion will follow you throughout your whole life until it's dealt with. While I was at The Forum I began to see how much of my life I had spent being a victim. If I got 'in trouble' I was a victim. If someone was 'mad at me,' I was a victim. If I 'did something wrong' I was a victim. Our leader said, "You victims are worse than the bullies. You go out and try to dominate the bullies and make them wrong." I sat in my chair stumped. I began to recall my experience of being molested. I was able to locate that from that circumstance on, I created myself as the victim. And then I began to see the cost of being that way. It cost me the freedom to be me, to have full self expression and connection. I decided at that point I was done with it.

One of the things of getting complete with the past is about forgiveness regardless of what someone else has done. From things that have happened there is always a way of being that we have that needs to be owned. In Landmark they draw lots of circles, and one of the exercises involves drawing circles separating 'what happened' from 'the story'. 'What happened' are the actual facts of what happened and the 'story' is all of the meaning we give to what happened (all of the things that we make up about what happened). The meaning I gave being molested was that I was a victim. The fact (what happened) is that I was molested. The story I made up about myself is that I was the victim. This was not the truth.

As I sat in those chairs and was listening to people forgive others, I started to ask myself he question, "Do I need to call Paul, the babysitter, and forgive him?" And of course the answer was yes. I knew it was time to forgive him for what he did so that we could both be free. I searched for him on my smartphone. His name showed up on the registered sex offenders page and the criminal background search. There were five phone numbers and an email address for him. I called all five numbers, all of which were disconnected. It felt so freeing to be ready to say I forgive you. A couple of months later I sent him an email and just told him that I forgave him for what he did to me when I was 7. I told him that I hoped he had lived a really nice life and that he was doing well. I knew that no matter what he did to me, his sister or anyone else, I wanted him to know he was free from any resentment I had toward him. He had the right to be forgiven and to be free.

Once I hit send I felt a huge weight off my shoulders. The email coincidentally bounced back to me a couple of minutes later and it didn't matter to me. I really felt free. I didn't need to hold on to this anymore. It wasn't benefiting me or him. "The truth sets you free," as Jesus once said. I was free. I no longer needed to play out my life as a victim. Now that I can see what happened as fact, I didn't need to continue to keep the story alive that I was a victim.

That's not to say that I haven't had times since then where I have taken on the role of the victim. My work has been to catch myself in the act of being a victim (to stop myself) and to say to myself that being molested happened when I was 7 and I am carrying on today as though I am still being molested if I am acting the victim role. I now know that I have a choice in the matter. I didn't when I was 7 and I do now. That change of mindset has been healing and freeing for me. And I know in the end that because I am free I allowed Paul to be free.

Landmark is so incredible--I can't say enough amazing things about it. The results that are produced in this short amount of time are mind boggling. This program works because it sheds light on things that one doesn't know about oneself. For me it has been such a source of healing and way to clean up relationships and live with integrity. And it is such a wonderful complement to all of the transformational work I have done with Baptiste Yoga.

After completing the Forum I did a ten week seminar on communications, I did the Advanced Course and The SELP (Self Expression and Leadership Program), which completed the Landmark Curriculum for Living. I also went on to do both of Landmark's Communications Courses, *Access to Power* and the advanced Communications Course, *Power to Create*.

The Self Expression and Leadership Program (SELP) was a four month course where we worked on developing a project. I went into the program wanting to grow Yoga for the Big D: Transform Anxiety and Depression through Yoga. While I was in this program I changed the name from Yoga for the Big D to the Wholeness Yoga Project. I also brought on Twyla to co-lead the Wholeness Yoga Project with me. It was wonderful to collaborate with her. I have traveled to Georgia twice and to Florida to teach and share the Wholeness Yoga Project by myself and have co-lead two four week Wholeness Yoga Project series with Twyla and we co-taught a workshop at The Eagle Yogafest in Eagle, Colorado in 2015.

Not only did I create a program to help others who struggle with anxiety and or depression, I got access to healing my own mental health. During the SELP, there were a few Saturday workdays at the Landmark Center in Denver. I partnered with a woman on one of the Saturdays and we were asking each other questions about the past. I realized that I wanted to attempt to wean myself off of Neurontin and I was extremely scared to do so. My partner helped me to see that my fears of going off of Neurontin were all based on the past. The goal with the work in Landmark is to view things from NOTHING!--to have no attachment to the past--to get complete with your past and don't fret about the future because it hasn't happened yet. Toward the end of the SELP course I began to wean myself off of Neurontin. I felt scared and yet I knew it was time to do it.

Replacing Medication with Self Care

Despite being scared to go off the medication, I knew in my heart of hearts it was time. I was tired of living in fear of the 'what ifs.' What would happen if I didn't have my medication? What would happen if I went off of it? Even though Neurontin had worked for me for a period of time, it wasn't working that well anymore, as I wasn't sleeping the greatest and I had plenty of mood swings.

I had discussed weaning off Neurontin previously with my family doctor. She told me that it was important to wean off over a period of time, rather than going off cold turkey. In August of 2014 I began to wean myself off Neurontin. The weaning process took me six weeks. Initially I was scared and I kept telling myself to stop relating to myself from the past and start creating myself from right now.

During the weaning process I starting using essential oils topically as a healthy alternative to the medication. Many of the oils are good for mood and also aid with relaxation and sleep. In addition to the oils, my yoga and meditation practice were going to be more important than ever. Just as one would take a pill everyday, practicing yoga and meditating everyday are essential to my well being.

It hasn't always been easy being off of medication. I definitely have to do the work to stay healthy. My self care checklist is long. My goal is to do at least half of the following self care practices each day.

- Meditate in the am
- Essential Oils
- Yoga
- Time in Nature
- Exercise
- Yoga Nidra
- Connect with friends and family
- Read
- Healthy Eating
- Practice sleep hygiene (see Appendix 2)

- Take a Tub
- Breathe
- Meditate in the pm
- Pray

Conclusion

This book could go on forever. I know that there will be dark days and light days. One cannot exist in the light without the dark. I know that I have the tools to be able to handle anything that comes my way. There will always be a new tool that I am learning to incorporate into my life.

The aim of this book is to be a source of inspiration. The intention of the book is for me to share my stories, to show where I have been in my life, and some healing resources and techniques that I have found along the way. I do not claim to have all the answers or even a fraction. All I do know is that there was a time in my life when it seemed as though I would never get better. And what I want to share is that there is ALWAYS hope. The kind of hope I am talking about is not where one sits around waiting for something to happen. It is having a strong faith in knowing that there is ALWAYS the possibility of change, especially if one is willing to do the work.

Hold on to what you believe in, whether you are the one struggling or someone you know is. Never give up. Keep your eyes on your true north star, even if your vision is blurry at times. You don't even need to see the star, just believe, trust and have faith that it is there.

Appendix 1: Facebook Posts

Here I have compiled some of the 'vulnerable' Facebook posts that I generated over the time period while writing *Bye-Polar* as a way to come out of hiding. Each time I got vulnerable and shared these with the world a piece of me got freer and in turn I offered that freedom to others. It's really true that the truth sets one free.

Facebook Post 1.29.16. Recently I have been getting constant reminders of what I have control over and what I do not. Last week when I got to the Denver airport my flight to Nashville had been cancelled and it wasn't looking hopeful to fly out that day. I had been dropped off at the airport on a shuttle. My home was 2 hours away. I felt trapped. There was nowhere to go and nothing to do. I called Tom crying about this, which is something I never do. I felt so helpless and powerless. Tom said, "Julie, you always go, go, go and do, do, do. This situation is telling you to just be, be, be." What great words of wisdom. With that, I let go, bought a cheap one way ticket to Nashville and made it.

While I was on the plane to Nashville, there was a mother who had two small boys, an 11 month old and a 4 year old. I could sense her tension. The baby screamed for over an hour. I thought I was going to lose my mind. I was riddled with judgment. Saying to myself, 'doesn't this woman know that panicking with a crying baby makes it worse? Why isn't she giving that baby a bottle or a pacifier. Can't she see that his ears hurt?' Then it hit me--I have absolutely no control over this situation whatsoever. I can either sit here and judge or I can be part of the solution. I asked the mother if she needed some help. She instantly said yes and I could see immediate relief in her eyes. Turns out that this woman was leaving an abusive husband who she said left them for dead the day before. She had no food for her children and was in a pretty rough mental spot.

I held that baby for over an hour and he was as good as gold. I got an apple juice from the flight attendant and had the baby drink it out of the can since there wasn't a bottle. She had no snacks, so I bought her and the kids some snacks. All was calm. This was probably one of the most powerful things I have experienced in my life. To be able to go from judgment, frustration and anger to love, acceptance and peace. It felt amazing to be *at cause* for this situation rather than *in reaction* to. Knowing that each moment in my life I have a choice. I am in choice of who I am, of how I want to show up and play on this planet. Each moment is a chance to give up control and to see what beauty actually lies right in front of me.

Facebook Post 2.16.16. My relationship with fear is crazy to me and yet not so crazy. Sometimes I feel so surprised that fear seems to have such a tight grip on me and yet when I look at the big game I am playing in my life it's no wonder that I experience fear from time to time. I know that fear is made up; it comes when I am not present in my body, when I am thinking about the future or the past. I know that my mind is the most excellent time traveler. My mind takes me to exotic places in the future such as on the beach, basking under the Hawaiian sun, and other times the time traveler takes me to dark holes, where the world is a lonely place and death is right around the corner. In yoga it's almost cliche how much we talk about being present. Get present to your breath, to where you set your eyes, to where your physical body is placed on your mat. And yet, sometimes, the time travel takes place. Sometimes it's a journey to the past. Sometimes that backwards time travel is really fun. I get to relive some of the best moments in my life--laughs with old friends, the Hawaiian beach, an awesome yoga training I did. And sometimes those backwards time travels take me to dark places...to judgment of myself and others, to reliving an icky conversation, or to regrets with the words I shouldn'ta, couldn'ta.

I am realizing at my ripe ole age of forty-six that I allow uncertainty to ruffle my feathers. With uncertainty comes fear and with fear time travel sets in. What happens when I am present to my breath, to the intention of where I set my eyes--my external focus and my internal focus? What happens when I am a YES? What happens when I put my attention ON what I want to have happen and be for it? I don't have the answers for everything, but one thing I do know is that if I put my attention ON what I want to have happen, then everything around me will conspire to creating what I want. If I give up what is constraining me and come from I am ready now, right now is all I've got, then I know I am traveling in the right direction, despite not knowing the outcome.

Facebook Post 4.8.16. "Oh the Places You'll Go..."

When I received this book after graduating from college in 1994 I had no clue where life would take me. All that I knew is that I was going to take a 'year off,' work at the Y Camp in Estes Park for my 4th summer, do NOLS (National Outdoor Leadership School) in the fall and who knew what for the rest of the year. While I was on NOLS my parents moved to Vail permanently. After NOLS finished in December 1994, I went to Vail, saying to myself, I am not staying. I will move to Steamboat, Colorado. As January 1995 rolled around I decided I would stay in Vail for the rest of the ski season. I got a job as a Vail Lift Operator. I met Tom in the Spring of 1995. I have done many things since then. I was on Vail Ski Patrol, I worked at Meet the Wilderness, taking at risk youth backpacking, I worked at Camp Vail, I owned a gardening business named Bedwetters, I became a wife, I became a mom, I experienced great joy, I became a mom again, I experienced great loss. I started doing yoga, I started teaching yoga, I opened up a yoga studio with a partner, I became the sole yoga studio owner, I have felt great sadness, I have experienced great joy, I have felt anxious, I have felt content, I have felt happier than I have ever felt in my whole life, I have felt depressed, I have felt restless, I have wanted to quit and give up many times, I have wanted to run away from everything. I have conquered some of the biggest challenges of my life. The places I have been haven't always been easy. I have stayed.

I reread this book three times today, twice to myself and once to my children. It has so many great parallels to life. There are ups, there are downs, there is fear, there is uncertainty, amazing things happen, scary things happen. And the last three lines of the book are this: "Today is your day! Your mountain is waiting. So...*get on your way!*" One thing that I know for sure is that despite the ups and downs in life I am committed to something much bigger than myself. This is what pulls me out of bed in the morning.

I have an incredible life that's worth living to the fullest. I want to leave a footprint behind that inspires everyone else to do the same. We only get one shot at this life, we'd better make it count!

Facebook Post 5.10.16. Last week I had one of the most powerful meditation experiences of my life. Initially when I sat my throat became tight, then it shifted to tightness in my chest, then it went back to my throat. The tightness in my throat felt as if someone's hands were grabbing my neck. I started to panic a little and then said to myself, "Julie, you know what to do." I took some deep breaths and worked the intention line from the crown of my head through the base of my spine and first filled it with love and then with compassion. Things slowly began to settle and the tightness in my chest ebbed.

I am not sure how the next part of my meditation began and I think I asked the question, "What do I need to do?" I heard this voice saying, "You need to forgive yourself." The next thing I knew is that I was face to face with my 17 year old inner child, sitting on the floor in front of the front desk where I was hospitalized. My 17 year old self was staring at the ceiling, catatonic and not moving. The person guiding me through my meditation said, "You need to tell her that everything is going to be okay." I Said, "No." The voice said again, "You need to tell her that everything is going to be okay." I said "No" again. The voice said again, "You need to tell her that everything is going to be okay." I started crying and said, "I can't tell her everything is going to be okay because it's not okay. Everything's not okay." The voice said, "Look at her. She is alone and scared and needs to be told that everything is going to be okay." So I succumbed and said, "Everything is going to be okay." And I hugged her and rubbed her back. Next the voice said, "Tell her she has a gift." I told her, "You have a gift." He said, "Tell her she has a gift and her gift is to go out and share that with the world."

So I told her that. The voice said, "Tell her you love her and accept her just as she is and she's done nothing wrong." So I told her that too. I was sobbing as all of this was happening. It was such an incredible release. Once I was finished talking with my inner child I continued to sit and the voice said, "Julie, you have a gift. Your gift is to go out and share that with the world." I said, "I know. What am I supposed to do with my gift?" He said, "You are already doing it." I said, "Who is this speaking to me?" Silence. I asked again, "Who is this speaking to me?" Silence again. Until the third time I asked, he said, "I am your creator. I am in you and in everything around you."

This was by far one of the most profound experiences I have ever had. It was so powerful to sit face to face with my 17 year inner child. Recently I have gotten present to how often I have been living my life from an upset 17 year old girl. Constantly viewing myself from the lens that I am wrong. I've done something wrong and therefore condemning others around me as wrong too. There is nothing wrong. I am not wrong, others are not wrong. We are all whole, perfect and complete, nothing more, nothing less.

Facebook Post 5.17.16. It's hard to believe that almost twenty-nine years ago I was labeled Bipolar. I had been living with that label for years and would only share with certain people whom I really trusted and made those people promise to never share with anyone what I had shared of myself. It was like a death sentence to have that label; what would people really think of me if they knew the truth? When I think of all of the drugs I have been on over the years to pull me out of the deep funk I was in, it's mind blowing. And thank God for those drugs. Who knows where I would be today without those drugs. They pulled my out of catatonia and back into life.

I had been on Lithium for a while, then taken off during my freshman year of college, only to be put back on it a couple of months later. I had an allergic reaction to the sulfur in the Lithium the second time I went on it. Was hospitalized a second time for two weeks. It was then that the doctors had confirmed that I was Bipolar. I resigned myself to living with that label for many years, despite not accepting it.

When I was taken off of Lithium, I was put on Tegretol, a drug designed for people with epilepsy and it also was a mood stabilizer. It was a great drug. I had no side effects and it kept me 'pretty sane' over the years. I was always told that if I wanted to have children, I would have to go off of Tegretol to prevent neural tube defects.

Weaning off Tegretol was the scariest thing I had done. I was terrified of going back into a deep depression and never wanted to go back there, ever! And I really wanted to have children. My desire to have children won over my fear of going off of medication. And so I had two children. I made it through two pregnancies and two postpartums, all without medication. At some point during that time, my shrink removed the Bipolar label from me. He said, “You are not Bipolar. You just struggle with anxiety and depression.” I was like, really? It’s that easy? I have been wearing this label around for years and you just took it away?

What the hell are labels anyway? They just put us in a box, confine and restrict us. A few months ago I was looking at my Follow My Health app (an online tool that provides access to personal health records) and it indicated that Bipolar was still active in my file. I messaged my doctor and asked her to make it inactive and I thought she did, until I looked at it today and it still says active. I am not sure how I feel about that. I know that I am not Bipolar. I know that I am not a label. I am me and I am free to be me.

If you are quick to label yourself or others, I invite you to step out of that. We are who we create ourselves to be. Others are who we create them to be. Words have a ton of creating power. What are you creating today?

Facebook post 1.27.17. Today marks day 20 of 30 days of no drinking. I am not drinking for 30 days for a couple of reasons.

1. It was recommended by a friend who's a doctor, to go 30 days, no booze in an effort to get my hormones under control. No drinking alcohol, along with no caffeine & taking some vitamins & supplements.
2. The second reason is that my spiritual healer, TeriLeigh, agreed with my doctor friend to go 30 days no alcohol and her spin was slightly different. In a healing session this past December with TeriLeigh I told her about my doctor friends recommendation of no alcohol. I also shared with TeriLeigh that I wanted to fully accept all of my struggles with my mental health. TeriLeigh said, "Your mental health monster is your friend. You use all your tools, you do everything

right, and yet you do it out of fear your mental health monster will take over again. It's time you start looking at the monster as a friend, who reminds you to keep your tools in place. When he gets loud you respond. That's the time to say Thank You. You are close to making this shift. I think that shifting your relationship with alcohol will be the last thing you need to do before you are no longer afraid of him, and you find him as your friend.

Facebook Post 1.30.17. While I was meditating on Sunday 1.29.17 I asked my higher power to show me how to make friends with my monster. I also asked what I ought to name him, since that was suggested by Amy Dawson on Facebook. So I sat and asked for names. I thought of Samadhi, the last of the eight limbs which means oneness or I like to think of it as nothing. There is nothing in the way between me and someone or thing else. So the name Samadhi was it. As I sat there in meditation I asked Samadhi to show me how to accept him and and have him as my friend. Miraculously he began to talk to me. He said, "The more you fight me the louder I will be. When you learn to relax and be with me the quieter I will be." I started to cry and I told him that I was mad at him for making me go through what I went through with all of my depression. He said you were meant to go through that. Those experiences were meant to teach you something and they made you who you are today. I agreed. He repeated himself a few times and said, "The more you fight me the louder I will be. If I am loud then you need to say to me, I know you have my back and I trust you." He kept repeating that too. "Say to yourself, I know you have my back and I trust you." It was as if all of the answers I was ever looking for were in that meditation. I know I am always quoting Baron Baptiste saying, "Whatever you resist, persists." I know this on a cognitive level and yet to be able to speak directly with my depression, “my monster,” Samadhi, was so freeing. I am excited to foster this new relationship rather than fight it. I know that this is the path to true freedom: developing a relationship with the darker parts of myself.

Appendix 2: Sleep Hygiene*

Getting sleep is as important as having proper nourishment as it allows space for mental and physical wellbeing. This sleep hygiene guideline was created by my friend Meredith VanNess who supported me during the Yoga for the Big D series.

1. Regular Sleep Time. Establishing a regular sleep/wake schedule is very important, especially a regular time of arising in the morning with no more that +/- 1 hour from day to day, including weekends. Time of arising is an important synchronizer in natural rhythms. Do not spend long periods of time in bed in the morning either.
2. Proper Sleep Environment. Avoid temperature extremes in the bedroom, either too warm or too cold. Too warm can disturb sleep. Make sure bedroom/house/outside environment is not too noisy. If so use a sound machine. Do not go to sleep with the television or radio on. Blue

Screens are stimulating. As a rule of thumb, turn off all media (computer, phone, TV) at least 30 minutes prior to going to bed. Ambient light can affect sleep. Use heavy blinds or an eye mask to shelter light.

3. Wind Down time. Stop working at least 30 minutes prior to sleep. In addition, do something non stressful, reading, writing, listening to music. Meditate for 5-30 minutes before bed to calm the mind. Do a calming practice such as a forward fold, legs up the wall and breath work to relax.
4. Avoid Caffeine. Caffeine is disruptive of sleep and can interfere with sleep patterns. Do not drink caffeine after 12:00 pm and even consider going caffeine free for maximum result.
5. Avoid Alcohol. Limit alcohol to 1 drink per night. Large amounts of alcohol can disrupt sleep patterns and not allow you to get into a full REM cycle.
6. Snack before bed/tryptophan. Some snacks can induce sleep before bedtime. Dairy products and

and turkey, banana, glass of milk, may help onset sleep. With that said, avoid eating heavy meals after 8:00 pm.

7. Regular Exercise. Periods of at last 20-30 minutes at least 4 days per week. Do not exercise within 3 hours of going to bed, unless restorative yoga.
8. Do not lay in bed worrying. After 20 minutes of not sleeping, get up, complete a short task & then go back to bed. Listen to a 10 minute yoga Nidra podcast. Do legs up the wall or a forward fold.
9. Deep Breathing. Counting and relaxation exercise as soon as you get in bed.
10. Do not take naps. Napping will interfere with your natural rhythm of sleeping. If tired in the afternoon, do 10, 20 or 30 minutes of Yoga Nidra, or read a book for 30 minutes to relax.
11. Refrain from drinking alcohol 3 hours before bed.
12. Eat a healthy diet full of colorful veggies and fruit.

13. Only use bedroom for sleep and sex.
14. Avoid clock watching. Turn clock away. Consider covering the bright digital lights with a cloth.
15. Start wind down time and bedtime rituals one hour from bedtime.
16. After 20 min of not sleeping, you can also try a meditation or breathing or relaxation technique or yoga nidra in bed before getting out of bed.

*Adapted from Meredith VanNess, LCSW, a Sleep Science Coach, specializing in CBT-I-Cognitive behavioral therapy for insomnia.

Bibliography

- Mayo Foundation for Medical Education and Research (2018). Bipolar Disorder. [online] Mayoclinic.org. Retrieved Apr. 25, 2018, from *https://www.mayoclinic.org/diseases-conditions/bipolar-disorder/symptoms-causes/syc-20355955*
- Seroquel XR (2018) Drug information retrieved Apr. 25, 2018 from *https://www.seroquelxr.com/bipolar-disorder/what-is-bipolar-disorder.html* and *https://www.seroquelxr.com/bipolar-disorder/bipolar-depression-symptoms.html*
- Wikipedia, The Free Encyclopedia, *Mt. Lamborn*. Retrieved on Apr. 25, 2018, from *https://en.wikipedia.org/w/index.php?title=Mount_Lamborn&oldid=790023029*
- Brown, Brene (2012). *Daring Greatly. Gotham Books, New York, USA.*

- *Childhood Sexual Abuse a Mental Health Issue.* Retrieved on Apr. 25, 2018 from *http://www.heretohelp.bc.ca/factsheet/childhood-sexual-abuse-a-mental-health-issue*
- Baptiste, Baron (2004). *40 Days to Personal Revolution.* Fireside Books, New York, USA.
- Avia Venefica (2005-2017). *What's my sign?* Retrieved on Apr. 25. 2018 from *http://www.whats-your-sign.com/cow-animal-symbolism.html*
- Dr Seuss (1990). *Oh the places you'll go.* Random House, New York, USA
- *Is Depression Genetic?* Retrieved on Apr. 25, 2018, from *https://www.healthline.com/health/depression/genetic*

About the Author

Julie lives west of Vail, Colorado with her husband, Tom, their two children, Charlie and Catie, and their Golden Retriever, Nala. Julie owns Revolution Power Yoga, a Baptiste Affiliate yoga studio located in Avon, Colorado. She is a 1200 hour certified Baptiste Yoga teacher and a LifeForce Yoga Level 1 practitioner. Julie loves being on her yoga mat, spending time in nature, writing, skiing, road trips with her family and having fun with family and friends.

CPSIA information can be obtained
at www.ICGtesting.com
Printed in the USA
JSHW010201070120
3380JS00002B/2